Advance
Getting to the

John Renesch's book makes his personal journey into the future, a journey that has meaning and relevance for all of us. A remarkable achievement.
> —Warren Bennis, Distinguished Professor of Business, USC, and co-author of *Co-Leaders* and *Organizing Genius*

John Renesch courageously weaves his personal journey into the dynamic pattern of global economic change. This dance between inner and outer realities carries us into the future.
> —Patricia Aburdene, co-author, *Megatrends 2000*

John Renesch has created a work which I can say, from my own reading of it, will most assuredly serve the world—not just the world of business or non-profits or civic communities but, more important, our own personal inner world. I hope everyone will derive the spiritual benefit that I have experienced as a result of reading this book.
> —James Autry, author, *Love and Profit, The Art of Caring Leadership*, and *Real Power, Business Lessons from the Tao Te Ching*

John Renesch has become the lead participant observer of what is surely the most dramatic worldwide transformation in the history of this planet. He gives readers the essence of what we need to know to get through this transition with grace and service to our world and ourselves. He has distilled his personal experience with the wisdom of the thought leaders of our day into an essential guidebook for this historic journey.
> —Michael Ray, Professor Emeritus, School of Business, Stanford University; co-author, *Creativity in Business*

Insightful, provocative, a catalyst for individual and organizational soul-searching . . . John Renesch challenges the mind, heart, and spirit with his new book!
> —"BJ" Hateley, co-author, *A Peacock in the Land of Penguins: A Tale of Diversity and Discovery*

John Renesch has written a brilliant business book, a powerful and passionate page-turner which must immediately be read by every person who works for a living, from interns to CEOs, in every industry and profession. John's insights and profound prescriptions are as pragmatic as they are inspired, as practical as they are visionary. This book has the power to instantly transform the world, if we allow John's words to penetrate our minds, hearts, and souls.

—**Robert Rabbin**, author, *Invisible Leadership, The Sacred Hub*, co-author, *Leadership in a New Era*

The future is our choice and making that choice is our responsibility, Renesch asserts convincingly. But we need a new mindset to turn crisis into opportunity and overcome our cynicism and sense of helplessness. To prove it, he provides priceless lists of things each of us can stop doing and things we can start doing to bring about a revolution of the spirit.

—**Perry Pascarella**, author, speaker, and former editor-in-chief of *Industry Week* magazine

John Renesch weaves a compelling case for why business must lead the transformation to higher levels of consciousness and spirituality needed to solve our global problems in the 21st Century. He provides a practical prescription to bring about a new paradigm for the 21st century as well as practical keys to accomplish it.

—**George Starcher**, Secretary General, European Baha'i Business Forum

John Renesch argues with great passion and insight that business people can— and must— become active participants in designing a better future for the whole human race. He argues with heart, soul, and great powers of persuasion that business and social good can (and will) be reconciled in a 21st Century culture led by a responsible citizenry, responsible parents, and responsible consumers. And he demonstrates why business, as the most thoroughly globalized force on earth, can be a transformative force in creating a new consciousness and a new order. Challenging, well-thought out, and revolutionary.

—**Sally Helgesen**, author, *The Female Advantage* and *The Web of Inclusion*

An excellent book, integrating many approaches to doing business in a more conscious manner.
— **Peter Russell**, author, *The Global Brain Awakens* and
Waking Up in Time

If we leave our spirituality at home, and never take it to the office, we'll change very little in our world. John's book argues powerfully for business to play a leadership role in the transformation of our planet. It is an argument I can't resist.
— **Neale Donald Walsch**, the author of *Friendship with God* and
the *Conversations With God* trilogy

John Renesch clearly and, I believe, correctly argues that business practices must change if we are to pass on a good quality of life to future generations. His skillful blending of his own life-work experiences with the voices of many others who are raising concerns about the future today makes for easy reading and easy assimilation of a tough message — if we don't change our fundamental notions about what business is all about soon, we may do irreversible damage to the planet's ecosystems.
— **John Adams**, author, *Thinking Today as if Tomorrow*
Mattered, editor, *Transforming Leadership* and *Transforming Work*

The world, as John Renesch puts it, is at a crisis point. The choice at this point is real and it touches the lives of all of us. Business, being—as Anita Roddick writes in the Foreword—the most powerful force in the world, will have to make it. This book is an invaluable guide for businesspeople to face up to this unprecedented responsibility.
— **Ervin Laszlo**, editor, *World Futures*, author,
Choice: Evolution or Extinction?

A clarion call to business leaders, which if heeded, could change our world for the better.
— **Hazel Henderson**, author, *Beyond Globalization* and
Building a Win-Win World

John Renesch's work will have special importance for people interested in transforming business. It's always refreshing to see a scholar nudging business to look beyond the bottom line.
— **Ed Cornish**, President, World Future Society

Getting to the Better Future

A Matter of Conscious Choosing

How Business
Can Lead the
Way to
New Possibilities

by John E. Renesch

NewBusinessBooks
San Francisco

NewBusinessBooks
c/o New Business Communications
P.O. Box 472379
San Francisco, CA 94147-2379
Fax: 415-474-7202

NewBusinessBooks are distributed to the trade by
Ingram Book Company (800-937-8000).

To purchase additional copies of this book or inquire about bulk discounts for multiple orders, please contact the publisher at the address above. See information at the back of this book for additional products offered by the publisher and this author.

Permissions and Credits

The publisher acknowledges the following sources:

IW article "Design a Better Future" (see Appendix B) is reprinted with permission from Industry Week, (May 6,1996). Copyright, Penton Media, Inc., Cleveland, Ohio.

Domains of Reality reprinted with permission of David Berenson. Copyright 1999 David Berenson, Sausalito, California.

The poem "Lessons" is reprinted with the kind permission of its author, Kathleen Pratt. Copyright 1994, 2000 © Kathleen Pratt, San Francisco, California.

Photo credit: Front cover: Larry Rosenberg

Getting to the Better Future: A Matter of Conscious Choosing
by John E. Renesch

ISBN 0-9610228-0-9
First Edition
Second Printing August 2001

A Vision for the Better Future

... a world in which the global business community serves society in ways that are life-affirming, sustainable, humanistic and responsible for positively influencing the future evolution of humanity.

— from *The 21st Century Agenda for Business: A Global Resolution for New Corporate Values and Priorities*

Other Books Created by John Renesch

New Traditions in Business: Spirit and Leadership in the 21st Century

When the Canary Stops Singing: Women's Perspectives on Transforming Business (ed: Pat Barrentine)

The New Entrepreneurs: Business Visionaries for the 21st Century (w/ Michael Ray)

Leadership in a New Era: Visionary Approaches to the Biggest Crisis of Our Time

Learning Organizations: Developing Cultures for Tomorrow's Workplace (w/Sarita Chawla)

Community Building: Renewing Spirit and Learning in Business (ed: Kazimierz Gozdz)

Rediscovering the Soul of Business: A Renaissance of Values (w/Bill deFoore)

The New Bottom Line: Bringing Heart and Soul to Business (w/Bill DeFoore)

Intuition at Work: Pathways to Unlimited Possibilities (eds: Roger Frantz and Alex Pattakos)

Working Together: Producing Synergy by Honoring Diversity (ed: Angeles Arrien)

Elegant Solutions: The Power of Systems Thinking (w/Verna Allee)*

The Conscious Organization: Multiple Perspectives on Organizational Transformation *

* forthcoming

Dedication

Willis W. Harman
(1919 —1997)

This book is dedicated to Willis Harman, a friend, a colleague and a mentor, who passed on in January of 1997. I often think of how different my life would be if I hadn't met Willis in the early 1980s. Thanks to him, I found some work that was well worth doing and which I felt particularly and uniquely called to do. Willis is still very much in my life. There isn't a day that goes by that I don't feel his presence and influence. Thank you, dear friend. Your vision for a better world and your influence went far beyond your students at Stanford, your colleagues at SRI and the Institute of Noetic Sciences, your family, your friends, and the readers of your books.

President of the Institute of Noetic Sciences from 1977 to late 1996, Willis W. Harman previously served as social scientist at SRI International and was Professor Emeritus of Engineering-Economic Systems at Stanford University. He also served a term as a member of the Board of Regents of the University of California and was a co-founder of the World Business Academy. His other books include *An Incomplete Guide to the Future, Higher Creativity, New Metaphysical Foundations for Science, Changing Images of Man,* and *The New Business of Business.*

"We just may be the most well-informed, yet least self-aware, people in history."
   —Norman Lear, television producer

lessons

what do you do
to teach your soul to dance?
what do you do
keep it locked deep inside
a jungle burial ground 'neath the layers
of pain, choked by fear, muted by inaction
or do you set it alight
on the wings of risks unknown
to take flight into a neverland from which
you are guaranteed no returns
and may very well fall
what do you do
to teach your soul to dance?

what do you do
to teach your soul to feel?
what do you do
keep it blanketed by
false warmth of
security, cloaked in silence impenetrable
locked behind the doors of steel
through which no cold wind can pierce
and within which all die a slow, certain death
or do you peel back each cloying layer
hardened icy to the touch
blow a soft, fiery blaze
from embers into licking flames
sure to burn, blister and sear
even as the higher form is attained
what do you do
to teach your soul to feel?

what do you do
to teach your heart to love?
what do you do
wrap it in pages
of lovelorn poetry, songs unrequited
never read aloud to others, yet just to self
keep it chained to you, handed
only so far as the leash will reach and
yanked back to count the tally of each
slight, every perceived wrong
or do you open cracks and crevices
wide enough for others to enter, find
their own niche to decorate
with dreams and passions of their own
paint its walls with tender caresses, come
and go as they please
no locks, no tethers, yet simple
strength of centered embrace
what do you do
to teach your heart to love . . .?

— kathleen pratt (C© 1994, 2000 by Kathleen Pratt)

"Only changes in mindsets can extend the frontiers of the possible."
— Winston Churchill

Table of Contents

A Vision for a Better Future

*A world where everyone is a powerful
and creative, compassionate and loving
spirit in partnership with equals for
the purpose of spiritual growth. A world
in which our allegiance is to life and
we cherish the living earth. A world of
individuals who are universal humans,
and whose goals are harmony,
cooperation, sharing, and reverence
for life.*

—from *Genesis: The Foundation
for the Universal Human*

FOREWORD
by Anita Roddick
Founder and Co-Chair, The Body Shop International

In 1991 I wrote my first book, *Body and Soul: Profits and Principles*. One of my goals in writing that book was to proselytize the values we had established at The Body Shop in the hope that one day the cosmetic industry would wake up and realize that the potential threat posed by our company was not so much economic as simply the threat of being a good example.

Business has developed a horrible reputation for itself. It has mystified me that the business world is apparently proud to be seen as hard and uncaring and detached from human values. How in the hell can anyone successfully run an enterprise these days without caring? How do business people keep their souls intact?

Today's corporations have global responsibilities because their decisions affect world problems concerning economics, poverty, security, and the environment. Yet, while global business binds the planet in a common fate, there is no international code of practice, no agreement on mutual responsibilities. And so much *could* be done.

Business is a combination of human energy and money and to me that equals power. Business is the most powerful force in society today and it is that force that ought to be harnessed to effect social change.

In late 1990 I learned of a business newsletter published out of San Francisco. It was called *The New Leaders* and it dealt with important issues around the responsibility of business for the quality and survival of human life. Its goal was "to bring consciousness to business." Through that publication I came to know the editor and publisher—John Renesch —and even wrote several articles for the publication in the mid-1990s.

I also wrote some chapters for a couple of the anthologies John put together—*The New Entrepreneurs: Business Visionaries of the 21st Century* (1994), which he compiled with Stanford Business School professor Michael Ray, and *The New Bottom Line: Bringing Heart and Soul to Business* (1996). I'm also a big fan of a 1995 anthology he compiled with Bill DeFoore entitled *Rediscovering the Soul of Business: A Renaissance of Values*—probably my favorite, and a book I've given away to many colleagues, employees, franchisees, and friends.

I've been an admirer of John's work for nearly a decade now and appreciate his role in helping the business community own up to its responsibility as planetary citizens and custodians of life in general. Rather than merely throwing stones at the established status quo, he offers wisdom and opportunities for people in business to accept leadership and responsibility for a true social transformation, one that will prove to be immensely valuable for all the world's citizens, including those of us in corporate life.

I was recently reminded of the Swedish word for business—"naringsliv"—which translates to "nourishment for life." This is hardly the way most people think of business these days.

Sadly, the business world seems to think of itself as quite the opposite since, for the most part, corporations exploit, manipulate, deceive, and evade in pursuit of greater profits—the all-important and all-consuming mission for most of them. I am still looking for the modern-day equivalent of those Quakers who ran successful businesses, made money because they offered honest products and treated their people decently, worked hard themselves, spent honestly, saved honestly, gave honest value for money, put back more that they took, and told no lies. This business creed, sadly, seems long forgotten.

A short, readable book, this new work by John concisely offers a vision for new possibilities for the future of the world, a vision in which business can and should play a pivotal role. The most dominant institutions in the world these days are the multinational corporations, who posses the awesome power to lead us down either of the two paths John puts forth in this book.

When I started The Body Shop, I had a great advantage. I had never been to business school. I didn't know what I was supposed to do. I didn't know the rules. I didn't know the risks either. I just went my own merry way, working from my gut instinct. I honestly believe I would not have succeeded if I had been *taught* business.

I found that a bank manager is the last person to ask for business advice because he is only a "housekeeper" of money and he rarely "gets to grips" with an idea and how to promote and manage it. Unfortunately, in Britain the two are confused and so no one is nurturing new talent and bright ideas. In contrast to the U.S., we British don't have the culture of enterprise. We have too much respect for "business" as perceived by "businessmen"— which translates to just money, or the banks— and there's little willingness to put money into innovation.

The wonderful thing about The Body Shop is that we still don't know the rules. We have a basic understanding that to run this business you don't have to know anything. Skill is not the answer. Neither is money. What you need is optimism, humanism, enthusiasm, intuition, curiosity, love, humor, magic and fun, and that secret ingredient— euphoria.

In this book, John offers a vision of the future that embraces all of these qualities. His optimism knows no boundaries as we can expect many pleasant surprises, once we change our thinking about how the world needs to be.

He also points out what we are in for if we remain in our current mindsets, thinking as we have been for the last several decades, and merely sitting quietly and allowing things to continue. So while he conveys a vision that all of us can be uplifted by, he's also defining what he calls a "choicepoint" for all of us —a time to make a collective choice about whether or not we wish to achieve our full potential as human beings. All it takes is changing our minds—the way we think about each other, our companies, the way we do business, and the rest of the world.

I recommend this concise book for any businessperson who wants to be part of creating a better future for us all and for anyone associated with any such individual. John has clearly defined the choice we now face as a species, a choice that may determine whether we become an endangered species or rise to a higher consciousness and accept a destiny we've never even dreamed of.

— Anita Roddick

January 2000

PREFACE

This book puts forth a vision of a better world, a transformed world, that is far more than an improved version of what we have today. The better world I envision is, to coin a phrase, a "world that works for everyone." Achieving this new world is entirely possible, but its creation won't be achieved by any familiar process like constant improvement. It can be achieved only through a process with which we are *not* familiar.

The better world I envision is one that can be "co-created" by means of a complete transformation in our thinking or what can be called a paradigm shift. This transformation will be more than change; this transformation will be historic. Humankind will have never before witnessed such a massive shift in worldview — the way we look at and experience the universe we live in.

This book is small by conventional standards. It is small because getting to the better future isn't all that complicated. I said what I needed to say and didn't pad more text between the covers of this book to make it appear more valuable. Cluttering up these pages would only imply that transformation was a difficult task. It is not. It is as simple as changing our minds.

This book includes personal anecdotes from my life, tales of my own journey and how I went from *entrepreneurial cowboy*, locally focused on challenging little enterprises, to a globally-focused thinker and futurist who sees the possibility of a much better world.

I feel certain that many of my own experiences and "wonderings" are similar to those of others even though our backgrounds and processes may have been quite different.

In this book, I put forth an idea that some may initially think absurd—that the business community is the most likely candidate to lead us in this historic shift of paradigms. This idea may seem ludicrous to the more cynical readers whose concepts of business include all of the darker elements such as greed, exploitation, manipulation, and selfishness. For those of you who share this perspective, I ask you to open your minds long enough to hear my argument for business being an agent for social transformation.

As the saying goes, "cynics are disillusioned idealists." Most cynicism has been the result of failed visions, unfulfilled dreams, and thwarted expectations from the past. So, as another saying goes, "scratch a cynic and you'll find an idealist underneath." Continuing with this metaphor, I aim to "scratch" any cynics who read this book.

I have also included portions of other people's writings in this volume—people who have "earned their stripes" sufficiently to drive their stake in the ground and assert themselves in support of a new future for humanity.

While I hope that this book will stimulate or even provoke you into thinking differently, I also expect that you will see new possibilities in your life, your organizations, and your industries for transformations beyond what I might envision—transformations built upon a worldview of true possibility for a better future.

Starting with a wonderful Foreword by Anita Roddick, one of the real heroines of the sustainability movement and founder of The Body Shop International, this book dives into the opportunity that lies within the global crises facing humanity these days. Next we look at the economic imperialism which reigns so supreme. Then we look at choices, creating a better future, and changing paradigms. The role of business is examined next, followed by a look at where ultimate responsibility lies for the next step in human evolution. As an example of what small groups of people can do, I describe one project in which I was involved, offering it as a way for the reader to join this exciting phenomenon. Finally, we head for home, recognizing our ultimate human destiny as human beings.

Acknowledgements

Before we start, I wish to gratefully acknowledge all of those people who have inspired and continue to inspire me in my endeavors to grow personally and professionally. These include but are not limited to some people I have never met, such as Abraham Maslow, George Bernard Shaw, John F. Kennedy, Martin Buber, W. Edwards Deming, Jack London, Robert Fritz, Nelson Mandela, Vaclav Havel, Mikhail Gorbachev, and Peter Drucker. There are also colleagues who have taught me so much as I have grown as a translator of theories and concepts that were born in academia, making them more widely available to greater numbers of people. These include but aren't limited to Michael Ray, Peter Senge, Margaret Wheatley, Ervin Laszlo, Fritjof Capra, and Willis Harman, to whom this book is dedicated.

In recent years, I have learned to be more direct and provocative in my use of language, both in my writing and public speaking. This provocateur aspect of my personality has been inspired by such forthright writers as Gary Zukav and Rob Rabbin, who also happen to be terrific friends. Thanks, you guys.

I am grateful to have worked with all of the authors who have contributed to the dozen anthologies I've created in the past decade, for their willingness to learn from me and for what I was able to learn from them. There are over 300 of them so I'll not list each of them here, but please know that you are no less appreciated because your name isn't among those on these pages.

I would also like to thank each and every person I ever interviewed for *The New Leaders* business newsletter, while I served as Editor-in-Chief (1990–1997). There were about 75 to 80 folks, from all levels in organizations, big and small, who were incredibly inspiring to me and our readers.

There are a number of people who've been very instrumental in my personal development, growing as a spiritual person, and becoming a more conscious human being. These people include Abraham Maslow,

Buckminster Fuller, Rob Rabbin, Rumi, Sahina, Lazaris, His Holiness the Dalai Lama, Raz and Liza Ingrasci of the Hoffman Institute, Werner Erhard, Peter Russell, and David Berenson.

I acknowledge all of the members of "the between group" who have been a source of tremendous support and validation for me over the past eleven years.

There are some people who came through my life at different times along the way, resulting in some conflict. I shall not identify them personally, but I have grown as a result of those conflicts, been healed of the residual pain, forgiven them as well as myself, and I thank each of them for the role they played in my development and learning process.

I am very grateful for several people whom I consider "elders"— men and women who have blazed a trail that I joined somewhat late in my life after a thirty-year career as an high-flying entrepreneur. These include the likes of Warren Bennis, one of the world's elder statesmen when it comes to leadership. And Charles Handy, whose words inspire millions as a management philosopher. And Riane Eisler, from whom I have learned so much about the genders and the subtle nature and conspiracy of sexism. And gutsy Tom Peters, the bombastic management guru who is so open with his own process, not at all like so many "experts" who become so attached to work they did years ago. And Jeremy Tarcher, a sweet man, who has been a source of great professional support, as well as Angeles Arrien, a living example of grace and acceptance. To Steve Piersanti, thank you for your collegiality, support and unconditional friendship.

As friends and valued colleagues, I'd like to acknowledge the following people who each have a particular place in my heart in addition to those I've already mentioned: Jim Autry, Claudette Allison, Gary Zukav, Alan Parisse, Anita and Gordon Roddick, Sahina, Ted Long, John Scherer, Bert Berson, Joyce Peterson, Marycatherine Dwyer, Michele Scott, Elizabeth Bloom, Verna Allee, Vince Scarich, Herman

Maynard, Peter Turla, Tom Kuhn, Marie Kerpan, Sheila Woodworth, Kathy Kirkpatrick, Sven Atterhed, Rae Thompson, Tom and Pam Frame, Nancy Hollis, Seth and Marilyn Manning, Susan Davis, Rolf Osterberg, Bob and Fran Ruebel, Stephen Roulac, Angeles Arrien, Kaz Gozdz, Christian and Lea Andrade, John Steiner, Oprah Winfrey, John Vasconcellos, Sergio Lub, Lynne Twist, Paul Ray, David Korten, William Halal, Claudia Holmes, Jerry Richardson, Pete Russell, Steve Soskin, George Leonard, Michael Murphy, Perry Pascarella, Dee Hock, Ken Blanchard, Paul Hawken, Robert White, Judi Neal, Martin Rutte, Joel Kurtzman, Peter Roche, Solange Perret, Jack Stack, Eckart Wintzen, Chris Grosso, Gail Holland, Kris Knight, Sven Atterhed, Paul Hwoschinsky, Marianne Williamson, Roger Harrison, Stewart Emery, Norman Lear, Charlene Harman, Ervin Laszlo, Thomas Moore, Ray Anderson, Lester Thurow, Maureen Simon, and Rob Rabbin.

I am very grateful for the collegiality and support of those who took the time to preview the unedited manuscript for this book and provide me with their comments. It is always comforting to know that there are others who are willing to be used for a common cause. Specifically, these people are Patricia Aburdene, John Adams, Jim Autry, Warren Bennis, Ed Cornish, Bill George, BJ Hateley, Hazel Henderson, Sally Helgesen, Perry Pascarella, Rob Rabbin, Michael Ray, Pete Russell, George Starcher, and Neale Donald Walsch as well as any additional people who offer endorsements after this book goes to press.

During my transition from an editor/publisher in 1997 to a full-time writer, I have performed services for several clients,. I am very grateful to have had the opportunity to serve these people and organizations during this time period. I am richer for the experience and learned much from working with them. These folks include Christopher Laszlo and Jean-Francois Laugel, Mark Bryant and Triune Communication, Nedra Carroll and her daughter Jewel, Colleen Anderson, William Guillory and Innovation International, Kymn Rutigliano and Burt Reynolds, Carol McCall and the World Institute for Life Planning,

Bert Berson and Joyce Peterson of Berson & Asociates, Rob Rabbin, Larry Liberty, Robert White and ARC International, Alan Kay and America Talks Issues, and Alan Parisse.

I'm deeply grateful for the collegiality and partnership of all of those people with whom I worked to create "The 21st Century Agenda for Business: A Resolution for New Corporate Values and Priorities" during the first half of 1999. The original group of us who drafted this document and signed it before it became public property numbered over forty people from 16 different countries. We expanded to over 200 by the time the Agenda was publicly posted on the Internet in July 1999 (The Agenda is explained in greater detail in Chapter Six). Thank you, Team. Good going!

Thank you, Kathleen Pratt, for your touching poem which you have so graciously allowed me to include in these pages.

I would not be doing what I am had it not been for the late Willis Harman—my friend, colleague, and an important mentor in my life. Though he passed on in 1997, I feel his presence nearly every day. Thank you for "hanging around," dear friend.

Thanks to Chris Hegarty for suggesting that this book be written, and for the inspiration he provided me over twenty years ago when I first heard an audio tape of him speaking to a corporate audience on the subject of transformation—a radical idea at the time—and they were listening!

I'm very grateful to Carolynn Crandall of Select Press and Jim Schneider of Right Angle Design for their help in editing, design and publishing this book and to the Ingram Book Company organization for distribution. My gratitude goes out to Karla Keller, Dottie Koontz, and Kathleen Pratt who reviewed the galleys for this book and caught some major typos. Thanks to all three of you!

I cannot say enough about Anita Roddick. I feel honored that she has graced me so publicly by agreeing to author the foreword of this book. Thank you, Anita.

I am particularly grateful to a friend, teacher, and coach—David Berenson. From him, I have learned so much about myself, the way people operate and the way the world works. Thanks to his incredible skill and intuition, I have been able to shine some light on those dark shadows that lie within me and become more and more aware of different parts of myself. I also owe David my life and I shall be forever grateful to him.

I am incredibly grateful for my spiritual life, which continues to grow richer and richer, undaunted by seemingly unwanted incidents in my material life that arrive unexpectedly from time to time. While a relatively recent addition to my life, my cherished relationship with the Mother in all her divinity has become a major source of nourishment for my soul. I feel so fortunate to have this experience.

"Taking a stand is a way of living and being that draws on a place within yourself that is at the very heart of who you are. When you take a stand, you find your place in the universe, and you have the capacity to move the world."
— Lynne Twist, founding executive,
The Hunger project

INTRODUCTION

DANGER AND OPPORTUNITY

The Chinese word for "crisis" is portrayed by two symbols—one symbol denotes "danger" and the other translates into "opportunity." Most of us only see the danger when there's a crisis in our lives. However, with the understanding that opportunity co-exists with the danger, one can have an entirely new perspective while being in a state of crisis. I know that every crisis I've had in my life bears this out. As I look back at situations that

were life-threatening, career threatening, or reputation threatening— and all of these have happened to me—I became a better person, a more conscious human being, as a result of *most of them*.

Why not *all of them*, you ask?

Well, in some cases, I didn't see the opportunity. For the most part, those were times before I began examining my life, before I discovered that I could really change myself and, thus, my life experience in this world. Before I learned this and began my journey to a more conscious life, I only saw the danger in any crisis that crossed my path. But the memories of these crises stayed with me, providing me with the chance to return to those memories, if I chose, and use them to grow.

Once I began to realize how much I could learn and grow from *all* of my life experiences, the time delay between the seemingly negative event and availing myself of the learning opportunity decreased. Nowadays, the gap might only be a few hours or a couple of days. A few years back, it took lots of soul-searching and some deep introspection (or what I call emotional "spade work") to see any opportunities in painful or fearful situations..

Lessons from My Life

One crisis from my personal life was a particularly painful romantic relationship that ended in the mid-1980s. It significantly impacted my professional life and was a very difficult time for me. It took me several years and many therapy sessions to reach a point where I let go of the emotional attachments I had to this woman, particularly the "I've been wronged" refrain that we so often hear in country-western songs.

Years later, I saw the opportunity that had presented itself to me in this crisis. But I had been so focused on the negativity that I never saw the positive. I finally realized how much I had grown as a person, how my suffering had been caused more by my attachment to being wronged than by the actual experience of being hurt and real disappointment.

Another crisis occurred a few years later. There was a particularly unpleasant work situation—I was falsely accused of wrongdoings by a colleague. It was very painful and I became very indignant. However, I knew that one of the first things I needed to do was to forgive my accuser—not for *his* sake but for my own inner peace and good health. It took some time for this forgiveness to come about, however, chiefly because I had it in my head that to forgive also meant to reconcile, and I knew that I never wanted to "engage" with this man again. A good friend pointed out that I could forgive him without reconciling. The proverbial light bulb went on over my head—a giant "aha" came over me and that was the end of any resentment residue I was carrying.

I learned that forgiving others is an entirely selfish act.

A few weeks later, I was talking with a colleague who had been aware of the drama surrounding this incident and I heard myself talking about it from an entirely different place. Instead of talking about it as if some horrible thing had happened to me as he was suggesting, I was talking about it with *gratitude*. That's right—I was downright *grateful* for this having happened! It was a great surprise and a major lesson for me about the power of forgiveness.

If that "negative" situation hadn't occurred, I might never have jumped into writing and speaking about social and business transformation—a source of incredible joy for me. How could I hold any grudges for such a gift?

So, now I more readily recognize the opportunities in what look like crises in my life. But it wasn't always that way and, I suspect, it isn't that way for millions of others. Every day I hear people ranting about how they were wronged, or betrayed, or screwed and it would appear that, barring any stimulation for them to change, they will take their bitching and moaning to their graves. That is really sad, when you imagine how many ways they could be enjoying their lives and affirming growth, expansion, and consciousness. It's sad to see them remaining stuck in the past with their "story" of the unforgivable wrong done to them.

In a more recent business crisis, I was able to complete the forgiveness process within a couple of weeks—much more quickly that the incident five years earlier and even faster compared to my "crisis" of the mid-1980s.

So why am I telling you all this?

The Opportunity in Crisis

I shared some of my personal crises with you because I see an enormous opportunity in the crisis facing humanity today. Much like my own growth as a person, learning to see the opportunities in my personal crises, we as a society can take advantage of our collective opportunity in this crisis —a crisis we face together.

Like visionary futurist Buckminster Fuller's idea of "Spaceship Earth," we have reached a point in our evolution when we need to behave as if all of humanity is on a spaceship. A threat to any one of us is a threat to everyone. As Fuller said, there are no passengers on Spaceship Earth. We are all crew members.

We all see the reports and hear the news about environmental degradation, the disappearance of civility and community, the growing cynicism in the world and the countless other dismal trends facing us and our descendents. The list is endless. The danger is very real! There is a crisis of historic proportions facing humanity as we begin the 21st Century.

There is no doubt that we are seeing the end of the great American Dream. Everyone on Earth cannot have what we have. There isn't room. Things appear grim. That's the *danger* part.

What isn't getting a lot of play these days is what tremendous *opportunity* lies in this historic global crisis. There's an opportunity for humanity to evolve to a new and exciting level of planetary consciousness, a new level of community, a new level of sustainability, and a new level of getting along. This is an opportunity for a transformation beyond our imagination!

Transformations are not predictable. Predictable differences are called "changes" and I'm not writing about just plain change. Transformations are paradigm shifts, where things are believed to be one way over here and then…days, weeks, or years later…they are now believed to be this other way. But the "other way" cannot be accurately predicted or planned for.

An example is the 17th Century "reality" that the Earth was flat. Everyone believed it was, so it was! Eventually, after a century or so of controversy and ridiculing the "round Earth people," the consensus swung over and, voila! No one would admit to ever believing the Earth was flat now that it was proven that the Earth was round (or, more accurately, a sphere). I'll say more on paradigm shifts later.

Nowhere in this transformation is there greater opportunity than in the business world—to lead the rest of humanity in this revolution of the spirit, this refusal to cave in to the cynicism and separation so prevalent in the world these days. Nowhere is there greater opportunity for global leadership, responsible leadership for the whole of humanity. And who is better-suited?

Now, before you raise your cynical objections or get too defensive about what I just stated, let me make my case.

A Lifetime in Business

I have spent over forty years in business. I think I was actually on someone's payroll for a cumulative period of maybe 24 months in my whole life, not counting my student jobs in high school and college. Business and the free market system have been a part of my life for a long time. I have very high regard for business and the potentials it can reach. I have seen business people achieve miracles when they can operate in a free market system without the bureaucracies of government or other institutions.

I am convinced that if the business community can see the opportunity in this global crisis, the opportunity to lead the way in such a profound and historic transformation—beyond the imagination of our ancestors—business people will jump at the chance to do so.

There are some who will be quick to point out that "the business of business is business"—not "saving the world" or helping with global problems. Those are the "It ain't my job" people who steadfastly refuse to accept any responsibility for the crisis we all are facing. Any transformation will have to take place over the objections of these stubborn Luddites. But we don't need unanimous agreement. So why not seize this opportunity now?

The human spirit lives in all of us—gardeners, artists, poets, and athletes. It lives in everyone. It even lives in "business people." Those of us "in business" have merely, for the most part, adapted our personalities to fit into what we perceive to be a certain way of being—acting, talking, and thinking.

We acquired a pattern of behavior that distinguishes "business people" from athletes, or artists, or carpenters, or window washers. It's like we've put on the costume and makeup, and rehearsed the lines for our role in the play. But underneath this assumed personality—this part we are playing—lies a soul like all of the rest of humanity. While this soul may have been suppressed for a while as a result of acting, talking, and thinking like "business people," it nevertheless has its connection to other souls and longs for escape from the role it has been playing. Like a slave wishing to escape bondage, the soul longs to be free and will seize the opportunity when it sees the opening.

In the following pages, I will be writing for your spirit, your soul—not your mind, your resumé, or your persona as a business person. I'll point out the crossroads where we stand as a species and address our evolutionary status a bit. I'll bring in several respected thought leaders from academia and business to help me make my points and elaborate on the possibility for a new and better future for all of us.

Now, let's get started.

CHAPTER ONE

THE END OF COWBOY ECONOMICS

I've been in business all of my adult life. In 1955, at the age of 18, I invented an alloy wheel for hot rods. In the 1960s, a partner and I began an event production company and staged our own public exhibition shows in places like the Cow Palace and the San Francisco Civic Auditorium as well as the Oakland Coliseum and the Los Angeles Shrine Auditorium. In 1968, I started my own public relations and advertising firm.

I *loved* starting ventures that allowed me to create something from nothing—something that provided a service or a product for which people paid me. It was lots of fun, full of personal challenge. I was the quintessential "cowboy entrepreneur"—the person who sets a goal, assesses the resources available, and then uses those assets to meet the goal. Like the American cowboy, I was independent, individualistic, and a risk-taker. If I ever got bored, and I frequently did, I simply moved on to something more interesting.

It was a *great* life! *Then*—in the mid-1970s—something happened...

After twenty years of challenge, fun, and total independence I began to wonder *why* I was doing this. *What* was I doing? What did it all *mean?* There were so many problems in the world and I was all wrapped up in my tiny enterprises.

I began exploring my life, my purpose, and my destiny. I began what former Meredith Corporation CEO, now business book author and poet, James Autry calls the "examined life."

Of course, like most people who begin journeys of self-exploration, I didn't begin examining the depths of my inner self because it just seemed like a good idea. Like nearly everyone who starts one of these inward adventures, I found myself in the midst of a "mid-life crisis"— except mine came a bit early, at age 37. And, like many people facing similar crises, I embarked on this journey concerned about what a mess I might discover "down there."

One of the first realizations I had after I started looking at my life was that many of decisions about how life was supposed to be were conclusions that I came to before I was 13 years old! It occurred to me that I would hardly consider walking up to a pre-adolescent boy on the street and asking him for advice about how to run my life. Yet this was what I was effectively doing. I was nearly 40 years old, following a life plan mapped out by a kid. This insight gave me the incentive to proceed digging. So on I went.

I hardly expected the treasure chest of riches that awaited me, a far cry from the Pandora's Box I had expected. I was beginning to find the words of Socrates to be more and more true for myself—"The unexamined life is not worth living."

After several years of some significant and very intense introspection I decided to commit myself to something bigger than just me— something that might have some positive impact on humanity. I asked around, talked to some colleagues and friends, and met some very intelligent visionary people who were doing work that seemed "important" for the future of the world.

Willis Harman

Among these people was a man named Willis Harman. Before I met Willis, I thought "I" was going to do something really meaningful. But I was still in the mindset of the "cowboy entrepreneur." After knowing Willis just a little while, I started to realize that there were thousands and thousands of other people—from all walks of life—trying to make the world a better place.

Willis Harman had been a professor at Stanford, a futurist and social scientist at Stanford Research Institute (now called SRI International), and was well into what he called his "third career"—as president of the Institute of Noetic Sciences—when I met him. He had written several books, including *An Incomplete Guide to the Future*.

Willis was an ordinary man, although quite intelligent, incredibly curious, and very cordial. But he had a very focused agenda ever since his Stanford days when he had his own epiphany of sorts. He knew we humans were on the wrong track—acting as if we are separate from each other when we are all really interconnected, to each other and to a higher power of some sort. He was very sure that the future could be quite different from the way it was shaping up if we would only change the way we view reality, the way we think about everything.

The Relationship Between Our Thinking and Our Reality

As I continued my period of self-examination, I came to agree with Willis—to believe in the power of human consciousness and how our "reality" is the product of how we think. I learned about consciousness creating reality. I learned how *material* reality is the product of *immaterial* beliefs, concepts, and ideas about how things are supposed to be.

I began to see how consciousness is causal—how our thinking creates the reality we perceive and how that system reinforces itself unless something challenges the system, or the status quo.

I came to realize how our mindsets—our thinking, our worldview, our core beliefs, whatever you want to call them—create our "reality." I saw how a strong belief that something is true can have a major influence in how we perceive things in our lives. I could see how these perceptions, influenced so heavily by our beliefs, can form the basis for our experience. This completes the cycle whereby beliefs lead to perceptions that become interpreted into experiences that reinforce the belief. This way we create lives that largely comply with our beliefs. Hence, our consciousness "causes" our reality (the way we perceive/ experience it). And the system continues to reinforce itself as we live our lives *unless we challenge it*!

As I grew and learned, I began to see how the world and our experience of it could be very different if we changed our thinking. I saw how *my* experience of the world could be very different if I changed *my* thinking. This was when I began to see the true possibility of a global transformation—a new reality that we could never attain by projecting from the present into some estimate of what the future will be. After all, all the projected scenarios for the future were pretty bleak, even if the entire population of the world became aware of all the problems *today*! But through a paradigm shift—a true transformation in how we think about reality, each other, and the world—an entirely different and new reality could be brought into existence. Despite there being little consensus for this perspective, I *knew* it was possible.

At that point I decided that I'd much rather be part of the community of people helping to transform the world than be part of the crowd watching from the sidelines. I was also willing to give up my "cowboy entrepreneur" self-image and become a team player.

Of course there was plenty of freedom and personal liberty associated with being a free-wheeling independent entrepreneur. It was a quintessential independence. But what about the "group good"—the "commons" that we all shared and relied upon. Part of the difficulty I had in making this commitment—this decision that led to a very new lifestyle—was the conflict I was feeling between my desire to be of service to the "group good" and the apparent loss of my independence, my freedom, to which I had become very attached. I later realized that this is also the challenge of "federalism" whereby individual states seemingly lose some of their independence in exchange for being part of a larger group of states, similar to what's been going on in the formation of the European Union over recent years.

Despite this difficulty, I wanted to work with the likes of Willis and the others I had met during my inward journey. But I was *very* clear that I didn't want to work in the not-for-profit sector. I only knew business. Besides, I *loved* business. So, I chose to focus on the business community—currently the most dominant institution ever created by humanity as well as the venue where I felt the most comfortable. And, somehow, I found that balance between my freedom and independence and serving the whole—the "group good."

Making Money

In the early 1980s, I was in the real estate business. Our firm specialized in making lots of money for people who entrusted us with their investment capital. Many of our investors received as much as four times their original investment in just four years time—for an annualized return of 100% per year! And that didn't include the phenomenal tax savings that went along with real estate ownership back in those days.

My two partners and I were the primary stockholders of the company, which purchased investment properties on behalf of investment groups that we'd form and manage, taking a percentage of the profits that were earned by our investors. I served as Managing Director for the company. Inflation was double-digit; highly-leveraged financing was the name of the game and equity growth was extraordinary. At that time, the U.S. tax laws allowed incredible deductions for real estate, so investors could write off four dollars for every one they actually invested. We were all running fast and making lots of money.

Simultaneously, I was continuing to examine my life—a journey I began in the early 1970s. I was looking at why I was here on the planet, and what all this meant in the higher course of things. Making lots of money for myself, my partners, and our investors began to seem a bit shallow and parochial in light of the world's problems.

It was during this period that the nuclear arms race got about as crazy as could be imagined and I began to see the state of the world beyond our little enterprise. I soon became more globally conscious and decided that I might be able to have some effect on bringing sanity to the arms race, which represented one of the most insane and out-of-control systems we humans have ever devised.

On the Brink

My journey brought me to one inescapable conclusion about the state of the world:

Humanity is simultaneously on the brink of two major shifts: On one hand, we are about to pass a point in our evolutionary calendar beyond which our future will be inalterably changed for the worse; on the other hand, we simultaneously possess the ability to transcend this trend and leap to a new level of consciousness. Each of these prospects represents a choice we have to make as a species. We can choose to do nothing differently, allow this failsafe point to come and go without any action—and we'll end up where we are headed. This choice is founded on mass resignation, inaction, irresponsibility, and cynicism. However, we can choose a second option—to consciously transform ourselves and create the future we'd like. This choice is founded on action, responsibility, and wholehearted optimism in the human spirit.

As much as we might fear human extinction, and worry about the future that will be inherited by our children, grandchildren, and great grandchildren, we apparently fear transformation even more since we pretend it's *not* a choice we have.

A quote that best sums up this fear is a passage from Marianne Williamson's book *A Return to Love* (widely mis-attributed to Nelson Mandela). Williamson writes:

> Our deepest fear is not that we are inadequate. Our deepest fear is that we are powerful beyond measure. It is our light, not our darkness, that most frightens us. We ask ourselves, who am I to be brilliant, gorgeous, talented and fabulous?
>
> Actually, who are you *not* to be? You are a child of God.
>
> Your playing small doesn't serve the world. There's nothing enlightened about shrinking so that other people won't feel insecure around you. We were born to make manifest the glory of God that is within us. It's not just in some of us; it's in everyone. And, as we let our own light shine, we unconsciously give other people permission to do the same. As we are liberated from our own fear, our presence automatically liberates others.

Pretending we are inadequate is *familiar*, even comfortable in a masochistic sort of way.

There's much more to talk about when expressing concern and worry about over-population, violence, resource depletion, and so forth. We are familiar with this path—we've been on it for quite a few years and we are used to it. We're more comfortable living this way, just as an old coat may be comfortable even though it is threadbare and out of style. The transformation option is totally *unfamiliar* (and therefore uncomfortable). So it seems to remain purely conceptual. Why? Because we choose not to engage it seriously. We pretend it's *not* an option. Are we so afraid of an entirely new level of mass awareness and experiencing self-actualization? Is the unfamiliar, despite its promise for a better future, that scary? Apparently so.

It is time to end this silly pretense and stand tall for the full potential of the human being. After all, this is hardly the end of the evolutionary road for humanity. Surely providence has more in mind for us than being these busy little consuming machines we've become thus far in our evolution!

The Adolescence of Humanity

In many ways, humanity is like the modern adolescent. After all, we humans are a relatively recent addition in the overall scope of the world's evolution. Like problematic teenagers, we resist full adulthood and feel torn between our familiar childhood (the way things were) and our unfamiliar but inevitable maturing.

Like teenagers, we may mature physically, aging as a species on this Earth. But like many people who have reached adult age physically, we haven't matured mentally. Getting older does not mean getting wiser. We all have shining examples of this in our lives—the fifty-something man who still responds under stress like a pimple-faced teenager. Being "grown up" does not mean being an adult. Adulthood requires responsibility for one's impact in the world—a stage in the evolution of humanity we have neither reached nor accepted as a species.

Like adolescent boys and girls, we tend to "hang" with the same crowds, forming cliques—which we call political alliances. Sometimes we form gangs (although we might call them armies) as a defense against other gangs. We develop our own laws and rules, and adhere to them with tremendous loyalty, much like the Hell's Angels or gangs in the ghettos. We experiment with drugs, alcohol, sex, and all the other numbing-out agents that might postpone our eventual maturation, just like a bunch of teenagers on a Friday night.

If you have raised children, there was probably a time or two in their adolescence when you wondered if they were going to make it— if they were ever going to reach responsible adulthood, or at least some semblance of it. You could see them straddling a proverbial fence, where they could fall on either side—become a young adult their parents could be proud of or turn into total delinquents, rebelling against "the system."

In his Introduction to the World Future Society's 1999 anthology, *Frontiers of the 21st Century: Prelude to the New Millennium*, Howard Didsbury, Jr addresses the possibility of human species maturity. Founder of the Washington, DC-based Program for the Study of the Future, he writes:

> Within the immense range of possibilities for the human race both for good and evil, one idea may become increasingly appealing and hopeful. With a new century—a prelude to a new millennium—it may become desirable and possible to experience "enlightenment" for the entire human family, and lay aside the burdens of past historical wrongs among all peoples and achieve the maturity to forgive past mutual cruelties, injustices, and antagonisms and manifest the wisdom to forget them.

The past is gone...The future is another matter. It is an open field of possibility.

I look at politics and the gamesmanship that goes on in the hallowed halls of legislatures around the world and see the most immature behaviors. Surely, politics is an adolescent activity.

Organizational Immaturity

Veteran management consultant Larry Liberty has developed a model for identifying the behavioral maturity level of executives and managers in corporations. Liberty, author of *Leadership Wisdom*, has worked with hundreds of companies and nearly 50,000 supervisors, managers, and executives. He has identified lower and higher functioning adults as well as high- and low-functioning adolescents among the ranks of corporate leadership. Obviously, the maturity levels he is addressing are behavioral and not chronological, having little to do with people's ages. Liberty is writing a book on this subject, a topic I find absolutely fascinating. While I certainly could have guessed that there were many adolescents among executives, I was very surprised to hear Liberty's estimate that adult behavior in American corporate leadership may amount to less than 15%, leaving the vast majority of executives acting out their adolescence!!

Think about it. If we are still in adolescence as a species, wouldn't there be a preponderance of immature behavior in our organizations?

Former U.N. Assistant Secretary General Robert Muller adds some urgency to the need for we human beings to "stretch our minds and hearts to the dimension of the problems..." He writes:

> There is no shadow of a doubt that the present political and economic systems—if systems they are—are no longer appropriate and will lead to the end of life evolution on this planet. We must therefore absolutely and urgently look for new ways. The less time we lose, the less species and nature will be destroyed.

Muller's words echo the sentiments of many concerned leaders in the world who recognize the dangers in this global crisis and advocate "new ways." Yet, for the most part, people are going about their daily business much the same as they have been for several decades napping through one of the biggest crises ever faced by humankind.

Slow gradual degradation can go unnoticed, especially when we are bombarded with so many distractions. We are conditioned to respond to any *immediate* threats to our survival, such as the fight or flight responses of all animals. But slow, gradual change—even if it is unhealthy, contrary to survival and life-threatening—can go unnoticed and thus suck the lifeforce from the unsuspecting or complacent.

Planetary Consciousness

Ervin Laszlo, the prolific writer and compiler of over sixty books on social systems and human evolution, founded The Club of Budapest in 1993. To amplify the need for a new awareness—what he calls a "planetary consciousness"—he has attracted an impressive list of "honorary members" for the Club—prominent people who echo his concerns. These include people you might expect, such as spiritual leaders like the Dalai Lama, Archbishop Desmond Tutu, and others. But he has also attracted famous artists—musicians like the late Yehudi Menuhin and Jean Pierre Rampal, actors like Liv Ullman and Peter Ustinov, writers like Arthur C. Clarke, and political leaders like Vaclav Havel and Mikhail Gorbachev. These famous and well-known leaders add credibility to the ideas Laszlo advocates in his writings, thus promoting and facilitating the spread of a planetary consciousness—the primary objective of the Club as stated in its manifesto.

In his 1996 book, *Choice: Evolution or Extinction, A Thinking Person's Guide to Global Issues*, Laszlo writes:

> Given its dangers and its opportunities, life in a grand transition entails responsibility. If we maintain obsolete values and beliefs, we also maintain outdated behaviors. Our own persistence in outdated modes of thinking and acting contributes to such an unfortunate outcome.
>
> The call is to feel the ground swell underneath the events and perceive the direction they are taking: to perceive the evolutionary trend as it drives social change in our world. The call is for a new and urgently needed form of literacy—evolutionary literacy.

Laszlo, a Hungarian living in Italy, believes that the best hope for us to develop this evolutionary literacy is through planetary consciousness. He firmly takes a stand for the future of humanity as he writes:

> All this makes for a tall order but an imperative one. If it is met, the new world would not develop as a continuation of the present, nor would it head toward global breakdown or global dictatorship. A functional framework would be created for the survival and development of the whole family of peoples and nations on this planet.

Self-Actualization

All of this makes great sense if you agree with Abraham Maslow, known as the father of humanistic psychology who was also named as one of the most influential people on management science in the 20th Century by *Industry Week* magazine. Author of many books, including *Motivation and Personality*, Maslow created the Hierarchy of Needs, which has since become a standard for human resource executives, consultants, and practitioners around the world. In short, he asserts that people's needs continue to expand as each level of need is satisfied (such as food, shelter, sex, belonging, and so forth), ultimately working up toward individual enlightenment—or what he calls "self-actualization."

CHAPTER TWO

A MATTER OF CHOICE

For the first time in human history, conscious choice about the future is possible. We are now able to participate in the creation of our future by ending the pretense that we have to continue sleeping through the next great upheaval in our universe. Why not wake up? Why not take an active role in this great social transformation? Why not stop pretending that we can't or aren't capable? Just because we never have doesn't mean we can't consciously influence our evolutionary path.

British futurist Peter Russell writes about a coming "age" replacing the Information Age in the relative near future. It involves the explicit acknowledgement of consciousness. In his 1995 book *The Global Brain Awakens*, he describes how greater and greater numbers of people will be employed in fields that support and facilitate the development of human consciousness, eventually surpassing the numbers working in the information industry—a sort of "consciousness industry." He calls this great overtaking of employment the "Age of Consciousness" and estimates the passing point to be in the first third of this century.

In describing how the unfolding of this new "age" could come about, Russell writes:

> ...the lag between the less-developed nations is steadily decreasing, and it should not take as long for the less-developed nations to move into the Information Age as it did for the West. We could likewise expect them to move into the Consciousness Age that much more rapidly, in which case the development of consciousness could well become the dominant human activity over much of the planet within the next century.
>
> In fact, the transition could happen even more quickly than this. First, those who are at present working on inner development are doing so in the context of a predominantly materialistic, externally oriented culture. They are pushing against the inertia of the old consciousness. As the proportion of people reaching higher states of consciousness increases, this inertia will decrease, and at the same time a supportive momentum in the new direction will start building up. The net effect might be that people would begin to find it easier to make progress on the inner path.

Russell adds another factor to the possibility of such an increased rate of global transformation:

> The second reason why the transition could come much more rapidly is that we may not have to wait for the majority of a population to be pursuing the transformation of consciousness before we feel the effects. It could be that a small number of people in higher states of consciousness would have a disproportionate positive effect on the rest of society.
>
> Such efforts could occur if one person's state of consciousness had, in some way, a direct effect on another's. Strange as this notion might seem, it is not totally implausible; indeed, there is growing evidence that it is happening all the time.

Of course, such a Consciousness Age can also have many other lasting effects, such as bringing legitimacy and credibility to the notion that we humans create our reality and that consciousness is causal.

This "consciousness of consciousness" will happen *with our full participation*, when we wake up, invite it in, surround ourselves in its new wisdom, and take full responsibility for whatever we might create. This means ending the pretense. It means we stop pretending that we don't know what to do.

Conscious Evolution

In a keynote speech to the World Future Society at their Ninth Annual Assembly in Washington DC in the summer of 1999, Barbara Marx Hubbard explained how each evolutionary step in social structure complexity is accompanied by an increase in human consciousness. Hubbard, who serves on the Board of Directors for the Society, pointed out that her observations were based on a reasonably long-term trend of some 15 billion years and added, tongue in cheek, that such a long-term trend could probably be relied upon (which drew a collective chuckle from the crowd). In her 1998 book *Conscious Evolution: Awakening the Power of Social Potential*, Hubbard writes:

> Deep in the hidden process of our metamorphosis we can see a natural design—an evolutionary pattern to guide us toward the next stage of transformation. We intuit the presence of the still-invisible butterfly, yet how do we become it? What we are seeking is a worldview that will call forth our creative action and direct our immense powers toward life-oriented and evolutionary purposes. That guiding worldview is, I believe, conscious evolution.

> Conscious evolution as a worldview began to emerge in the latter half of the 20th Century because of scientific, social, and technological abilities that have given us the power to affect the evolution of life on Earth. Conscious evolution...is the fruit of all human history and the opening of the next stage of human development...Conscious evolution...heralds the second great event in the history of the universe. We are not speaking of some minor new idea but of an advance in the evolution of evolution itself.

Hubbard examines cocreation as an element in this evolutionary shift. She cites the unprecedented ability we now possess to choose our own destinies and to partner with universal humanity to have what she calls a "cocreative society." She writes:

> The cocreative society occurs when this superorganism….this immense collective power of modern society is consciously and lovingly oriented toward the evolution of humanity.
>
> The cocreative society cannot be imposed or engineered into existence. It is nurtured into being by increasing the connections and coherence among those already initiating vital actions. It emerges when we collectively overcome the illusion of separation that has divided us, for the capacities we need—the technology, resources, and know-how—are already present in their early stages to realize our evolutionary agenda.
>
> The cocreative society may seem impossibly difficult from the historical perspective, but from the evolutionary perspective we are encouraged.

Creative Tension

Did you ever feel that what you wanted was as far from the way things were that you began to get discouraged? Can you recall the conversations you had with yourself about quitting or lowering your sights? Well, that was your mind wanting to relieve the tension.

Robert Fritz, author of *The Path of Least Resistance*, was the first person I knew of who described a visionary approach to creating a new reality for oneself. He called the gap between the way things are and the way we want them to be "structural tension." He noted that this tension includes an emotional component, which he's labeled "emotional tension," that includes fears that we harbor about our being able to manifest our vision. In many cases, he argues, this fear is based upon an inherent belief of unworthiness or powerlessness. Since tension seeks resolution, and fear can interfere with the vision being realized, the tension is most often resolved by lowering of the vision—or what is wanted—thus allaying the fear.

The way I first saw this demonstrated was with two hands, one over the other, with outstretched fingers, inside of a rubber band. The upper hand represents the vision, the way we want things to be, the future reality that we desire. The lower hand represents the present day reality, the way it is right now. As the hands move apart and the gap grows between one's desire for a better future and the present reality tension builds in the elastic band. Eventually, the hands are restricted

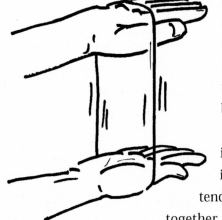

by the band and it takes a certain amount of strength to keep the two hands apart. The stretched rubber band provides a tension that is trying to bring the hands back together.

Due to this tension being imposed on one's hands and arms in maintaining this gap, there's a tendency to bring the hands closer together thus relieving the discomfort.

Similarly, people often lower their expectations for the future, their visions, and dreams for themselves and their loved ones, because of this tension. They choose not to maintain it. They assume that "reality" won't change so they must reduce their ideas about what's possible in order to lessen the tension. In the model of the two hands, they lower the upper hand. Their discomfort is relieved but their dreams are compromised.

However, if one assumes that their reality *can* change, tolerates the tension, and maintains one's vision, one's reality starts to shift. The lower hand starts to rise. The tension is still relieved but the vision is closer to being realized. The "way things are" moves closer to the "way we want them to be."

In Peter Senge's 1990 book—*The Fifth Discipline*—Fritz's model became more widely known as "creative tension."

Global Visionaries

From 1977 to 1980, concurrent with starting our real estate company, I offered one-day workshops in goal-setting. I was deeply immersed in the human potential movement and remember an adage that goes like this: You either have what you want or the reasons why you don't have it. I had a slightly modified form of this saying which went like this: You either have what you want, are heading toward it, or you have the reasons why you don't.

The principle for either version is that rationalizations stop people from achieving their dreams! Many people who took my workshops had great difficulty in setting any goal for themselves unless they knew how they were going to achieve it. This *greatly* limited their ability to put forth a goal! The power of the dream—the *vision*—does not require a blueprint for achieving it before it can be envisioned. All that's needed at the beginning is the vision.

Remember the now-famous vision John F. Kennedy put forth in the early 1960s about landing a man on the moon, without much of a clue as to the "how" we'd do it? He put it forth to the American people as a vision and—voila! We not only got there, but we did so ahead of schedule!

How about a large community or an entire metropolitan area, getting something they all want, undeterred by the cynics and the disbelievers? Large communities have been transformed out of the collective intention of the people, where "miracles" occurred and the cynics couldn't believe what the community had pulled off. Community revitalization projects for neighborhoods and urban renewal programs in big cities have been routine throughout the U.S. and the rest of the world. It is simply a matter of *collective intention*, which leads to generating the necessary resources and sustainable effort to complete the transition. But it begins with intention and a belief in the possibility that it can be done.

Now, imagine a larger group, like *all of society*. That's right, the *entire world*. The whole human community, including all the peoples of the world with all of their diversities, can muster a collective intention to transcend the conditions in which most of us live. If we can let go of all the reasons why we cannot do this, we can take the first steps in moving toward a sustainable, compassionate, and life-affirming world.

Visionaries need to be able to maintain that structural tension that Fritz talks about—that gap, between the way things are and what they could be—despite the despair and sadness and all of the other emotions that arise when things don't "improve" as quickly as they would like. People who cannot or will not feel their emotions and experience these "negative" feelings – those who cannot deal with that tension—are the followers, the people who will jump on the "new vision" bandwagon only when it looks like it has a reasonable chance of succeeding.

Remember, we can either have what we want, or the reasons why not. Which do you prefer? What do you want?

*"We are at that very point in time when
a 400-year old age is rattling in its
death bed and another is struggling to
be born..."*

— Dee Hock, founder,
VISA International

CHAPTER THREE

CREATING THE BETTER FUTURE

"The best way to predict the future is to create it." These are the words of Peter Drucker, globally recognized as the senior elder and father of management theory. The author of a couple of dozen books, including *Post-Capitalist Society, The New Society,* and *The Future of Industrial Man,* Drucker has enjoyed over half a century as one of the most influential people for the business community. So, if we are to create our future, why not create the best one we can? A better future will let business people see the possibility rather than just the uncertainty. They will hold a positive vision for the future rather than being held back by resignation and cynicism. This will require a major change in how we perceive the world—a paradigm shift.

Facilitating one of these shifts, where the existing paradigm's legitimacy is challenged, allowing a new one to take its place, is an exciting task. I've learned that I cannot make it happen by myself (though there was a time when I arrogantly thought I could). But I can be one of many who help facilitate it—if the field of possibility exists. And, right now, it does! If the business community can envision the possibility of a new world—a new reality based upon very different values and priorities—it will make an immediate shift in how it relates to society. After all, human beings have created no other institution that can change so fast and adapt so quickly as the commercial enterprise—standing ready 24 hours a day to adjust to frequent and erratic changes in a fickle marketplace.

The Invisible Revolution

Shortly after I realized that there was a growing consciousness about these issues in the business community, I coined the term "invisible revolution" to define that growing experience of restlessness and discontent that was percolating up through grassroots workers. I had little evidence for this revolution, which is why I called it "invisible." But I could sense it as a rapidly growing phenomenon in the American workplace and had strong suspicions that it was stewing in other industrialized countries as well.

I recall sitting in the Stock Exchange Club in downtown San Francisco, having lunch with a high-level executive from Bechtel, one of the world's largest builders of dams, power plants, and other projects of massive proportions. It was in late 1990. As we became better acquainted, I gradually took the conversation to deeper and more personal levels. I was careful not to pry too quickly—after all, topics like spirituality and consciousness just weren't talked about in most corporate environments. By the time lunch was over, we were finally able to address the "S word" (spirituality) as he called it—a word he'd never use at work because "we just don't talk this way there."

Many male executives have been significantly influenced by their spouses. This should be no big surprise since women buy most of the books in the U.S. and have been far more comfortable in matters of the heart and soul than men. Additionally, women have been starting more businesses than men over the past decade, so the influence of women in this trend has been quite powerful. But, to a male executive, particularly a middle-aged male executive, an intimate conversation with his spouse is very different from expressing himself about these things with others. And given that so many men value their work as a large part of their personal identity, you can see why they'd be quite protective of that identity. You can see why they'd be reticent to share anything really personal, particularly with co-workers or people they've identified as part of their professional community.

As the years went by, I noticed a growing willingness among business folks to include these topics in conversations—that is as long as they were private, one-on-one conversations. I also noticed the sales of books on the subject of spirituality and business started growing to the point where management guru Tom Peters focused on the phenomenon in one of his 1993 syndicated columns. I suppose this trend was partially due to the growing discontent with the status quo and the trends toward dehumanization, but I believe another factor was the vitality of the human spirit refusing to be squelched.

But this revolution was still underground, still not part of open and public discourse. It was still invisible.

That is, until the following year.

The Invisible Becomes Visible

In 1994, a San Francisco consumer research company—America LIVES—announced that they had discovered a relatively new subculture in the U.S. Prior to their findings, the major subcultures in this country were Traditionalists and Modernists. Neither of these two perspectives seemed to hold any real hope for a sustainable future. However, a new subculture of "cultural creatives" had apparently sprung up over the past quarter-century, and already represented about 24% of adults, or over 44 million people.

I was ecstatic! There was finally a sign that the revolution was becoming visible!

Sociologist and researcher Paul Ray has since written extensively about this new third subculture (sometimes referred to as the "integral culture") that endorses neither extreme of Traditionalists or Modernists. These people are far more receptive to the psychological, spiritual, and holistic approaches to today's problems. In a 1995 report sponsored by the Fetzer Institute and the Institute of Noetic Sciences, Ray writes:

> The image of the Integral Culture is precisely the kind of image that Fred Polack said modern society does not have, and would need to have in order to survive. He said in 1950 that the West has no image of the future at all, and that's dangerous. The West needs a cultural revitalization movement....but it differs strongly in that it seeks new ways to move off into the new, rather than to return to an idealized past, or to restore old ethnic or religious 'purities.'

> The Cultural Creatives were too few to measure one generation ago, and their numbers have clearly grown to almost a quarter of the adult population.

Ray's findings also include the ratio of women to men in this newly discovered subculture. Not surprisingly, women Cultural Creatives outnumber men by two to one.

Ray summarizes his findings by writing:

> Take heart! Unbeknownst to most of us, we're traveling in the midst of an enormous company of allies: a larger population of creative people, who are the carriers of more positive ideas, values and trends, than any previous Renaissance period has ever seen. And, they can probably be mobilized to act altruistically on behalf of our future.

Cultural Creatives represent a growing grassroots awareness that many old ways are no longer valid and must be abandoned or significantly modified if humanity is to take the next step in its evolution. This is the crux of humanity's next step—in choosing whether to continue unconsciously proceeding to an inevitable future or to consciously create a future of possibility. As Ray states:

> In the next two decades our world will either be dramati-
> cally better or dramatically worse. The one thing that
> cannot happen is just "more of the same." Most trends of
> the past are simply not sustainable. The era of obvious
> steps to progress is gone, and we face the Great Divide. It
> really could go either way: Our future is not foreordained.
> We are at a tipping point in civilization.

If we can reach those people who see greater possibilities for themselves, business, and the rest of society—business and society together can transform our future from one of continued degradation to one of hope and possibility for everyone .

After all, isn't the future of humanity worth some effort? Isn't it worth getting out of our comfort zones, individually and collectively? Do we really want to leave the future of humanity to chance and probabilities?

New Thinking Needed

Trying to get to a better future using the same thinking that got us here is fruitless. As long as we insist on staying in the same mindset—material, scientific, linear thinking—we will never transcend the conditions in which we find ourselves.

Einstein told us earlier this century that not everything that can be counted counts, and not everything that counts can be counted.

A transcendent or spiritual perspective is called for if we are to make this transition to a new age—an "Age of Consciousness" as Russell calls it. The good news is that it doesn't take any great effort to get there. The transcendent need not *replace* the scientific/reduction-istic perspective.

Reductionism claims that the physical is primary; transcenden-talism makes the spiritual primary. But there doesn't need to be one *or* the other. Both can co-exist without one being primary or dominant over the other

Contrary to the masculine-dominated scientific paradigm, there's not much "doing" needed. More "being-ness" is required than "doingness." What *is* needed is willingness, an allowing for the Divine to enter our consciousness—implicitly *and* explicitly.

Television producer Norman Lear talked about the explicit and the implicit. He made the distinction between being *informed* and being *aware* in an interview with human potential pioneer Stewart Emery in the 1994 *Leadership in a New Era*. Lear told Emery that:

> I find there is no conversation that isn't tangential to some question that relates to higher meaning and all the unanswered questions.
>
> I sometimes wonder if this isn't the root cause of so much that is wrong on the surface of our society. We just may be the most well informed, yet least self-aware, people in history.

There was another occasion when privately held thoughts became publicly explicit. In 1996, *Industry Week* magazine called me and asked to do an interview for their "On the Edge" series. My stance about consciousness and business had struck a chord with the magazine's former Editor-in-Chief—Perry Pascarella—who would be doing the article. The last person featured in this series was Francis Fukuyama, the author of *The End of History*, so I was quite flattered to be in such illustrious company. The interview seemed to go well and I was eager to see how the article would eventually be published.

I wondered if the magazine's editors were going to edit out much of what Perry had written, particularly those parts about higher consciousness and spirituality. After all, I was advocating consciousness and higher power to readers who were mostly manufacturers and technical folks who had a strong psychological investment in hard science and machines. I wondered if the headline for the article would put a cynical spin on the story. I wondered if the article was going to be placed in the rear of the magazine where few readers would even notice it. I've been around for a few years and I've seen many ways that editorial and production staff can reduce the impact of a story. It isn't just the journalists who can interpret and influence the way an article is received.

To my surprise, the interview was published as a four-page feature, complete with a full-page color picture, accurate quotations, and reasonably good editing considering the radical nature of the topic.

The article was headlined "Design a Better Future" and its publication provided me with enormous credibility for my viewpoint. I was not only excited for myself and my work but I was also very excited about the business world's receptivity of such esoteric ideas.

The full text of the *Industry Week* interview is reproduced in the Appendix. However, I'd like to insert a portion here, written by Pascarella:

> For Renesch, the world crisis is more than a matter of conserving resources. He aims way beyond preserving physical resources to engaging the human spirit. "The spirit is that spark that tells us we're alive. When work is meaningful, when one's passion is being involved in his or her work, there's a sense of aliveness, a sense of the human spirit thriving," he says.
>
> Environmentalists work to postpone the limits to consumption, but Renesch strives to hasten a shift in consciousness—a major transformation. "Too many of us are spending our time paying the mortgage, feeling the need to numb out in some way -watching TV, drawing way from people, substance abuse—just putting in our time. The American Dream has gotten really distorted," Renesch says. "It's a consumer-based dream. The American Dream of the founding fathers was very spiritually based. Somewhere after World War II, the American Dream changed."

Pascarella continues the interview, asking me why I think it's the business community's role to lead this transformation. Starting with my response, he writes:

> "I think it's appropriate that this country be the source of a renaissance of responsible business, because we are the first ones to see the downside of the dream," [Renesch} explains. Business is in the best position to lead a transformation, he is convinced, because it has a "disproportionate share of influence on society. With that much control over people's lives it's inherent—a kind of natural law—that you've got responsibility for it. In the days of Adam Smith in the 1700s you had a presumption that you had

a moral society. You had a presumption that there was a conscience at work. Over the years, we have done so much in the way of legislation and the rule of law that we've unconsciously evolved to a state of where everything is OK unless it's illegal. So there's no longer an inner moral code. The moral compass went out the window, and it became a game of exploiting loopholes. Our conscience has atrophied."

A television news anchor for the Fox Network recently commented that "bending the rules is the American way." How telling.

I might add here that this game of "if it isn't illegal, it must be OK" has contributed enormously to business's focus on the *form* of things, complying with regulations and the law, rather than the *spirit* of right and wrong—that "natural knowing" that tells us what's really just and appropriate under any circumstances.

Our Western Ways

We in the West have a number of propensities, some that work for us and some that work against us. One of them is our impatience—our desire to have answers to our problems just as soon as we can. Compounding this impatience is our familiarity with the domains of form and content—or the realms of the mental and the physical. This obsession has generated a near-fixation on these realms, contributing to their primacy in business, economics, and other aspects of our lives.

This pseudo-fixation also contributes to the fascination with evidence as our primary measure for what is real and what is not. In other words, if it can't be explained, proven by logic, or demonstrated to the five physical senses, it is at best suspect and at worse dismissed.

An example of how the West gets fixated on form can be seen in the work of W. Edwards Deming, now acknowledged as the man who facilitated the incredible transformation in Japanese manufacturing. The Japanese went from being known for their "cheap copies" or inexpensive knock-offs of Western products to being global leaders in high-quality production. Before his death a few years ago, Deming was finally recognized for the groundbreaking work he has achieved in changing the world's standard for quality in consumer products. But the road was bumpy. He only went to the Japanese after arrogant and smug American manufacturers rejected his philosophies.

After U.S. manufacturers, particularly the automotive industry, realized that they were getting beaten at a game they had dominated for so many decades, they became more receptive to new ideas about quality. Deming—the proverbial "prodigal son"- began consulting in Detroit (or Dearborn to be more precise) while companies throughout the U.S. jumped on the quality bandwagon. But, here's where the Western ways show up.

Instead of taking the time and the discipline to absorb the context or substance of what Deming was advocating, American manufacturers took a quick look at the Japanese plants and came home to quickly implement what they saw. "Quality Circles" cropped up everywhere. Months later, the quality movement started to slide into the trash heap of "flavor of the month" fads and trendy management gimmicks. Finally, someone got the message that Deming's work went far deeper than just Quality Circles. His work required transformations in how manufacturers saw their jobs. His work involved shifting the *context* of their work, not merely changing the *form* of it.

There's a contemporary colloquialism that sums up this short-sightedness, this constant hunt for the quick fix: "It's like rearranging the deck chairs on the Titanic."

Domains of Reality

The Titanic crew was complacent in their arrogance, believing that their ship was unsinkable. This complacency allowed them to be concerned over relatively trivial matters while taking the invincibility of their ship for granted. This was much like American auto manufacturers in the 1970s. The "Western way" of dealing with the form rather than the substance has its limitations. And, to some who are wedded to the American Way, this idea is pure heresy.

The East and the West have much to learn from each other. Certainly, the Japanese have learned much from their industrialized Western brothers and sisters. So have the Chinese and the Koreans. But what are we learning from our Eastern brothers and sisters?

Philosopher and consultant David Berenson has developed a matrix that makes distinctions among four differing perspectives of what is "real." He calls it "The Four Domains of Reality." The beginning of Berenson's matrix is shown below:

Domain #1	Domain #2	Domain #3	Domain #4
Context	Process	Form	Content

The first two domains—Domains #1 and #2, Context and Process—are seldom recognized in the West since they are intangible and, therefore, less "real" according to consensus thinking in the industrialized societies. As I mentioned earlier, we in the West have a tendency to value Form (Domain #3) and Content (Domain #4) over these first two domains and thus see them as more "real." The thinking is something like "if it can be measured, analyzed, or thought about, *then* it exists." Of course the opposite corollary is also accurate: "If it can't be seen or measured, it must *not* exist."

The Form and Content domains are where empiricism lives. And they feed each other like the blueprint, the idea, or the plan (Form) can lead to the final structure, product, or event (Content).

Berenson goes on to other levels in each domain, expanding their meaning. So, in the domain of Content (Domain #4) there also exists perception, the physical reality, and sensation. Similarly, in the domain of Form (Domain #3), there exists the conceptual, the mental, and thinking activities. Here is his complete matrix:

Four Domains of Reality

Copyright 1999 © David Berenson

1.	2.	3.	4.
Context	Process	Form	Content
Abstract	Experience	Concept	Perception
Spiritual	Emotional	Mental	Physical
Intuition	Feeling	Thinking	Sensation

The industrialized mindset of the West is grounded in the fourth domain—Content, or the physical domain. In other words, there's what "is" (Domain #4) and then there's what we think about what "is" (Domain #3)

Domain #2, where feelings, the emotional and the experiential reside, is unfamiliar to most people in the West. It is also uncomfortable for most Westernized people to talk about—especially for many men who have been conditioned to deny or suppress feelings.

In the past decade, I have noticed a huge gain in acceptance for process in business meetings, largely influenced by women's participation in the workplace. In earlier years, process was looked upon as "wasting time" and shouts of "let's get on with it!" could be heard whenever any processing got underway. And, usually, the shouts were from the men. Process has risen in acceptance as a valuable part of brainstorming, the creative process, and team-building, but only after overcoming some resistance from the bottom-line focused business minds.

The least understood and most ignored domain—the domain of Context, which includes the spiritual, abstract, and intuitive—is actually the generative domain, the source of all creativity, according to Berenson.

Context generates Process which translate to Form which results in Content. Said differently, the abstract generates experience, which results in concepts that lead to perceptions. The spiritual generates emotions that stimulate mental activity which manifests in the physical realm. Our intuition generates feelings which, in turn, evoke thinking that leads to sensations.

So, there is a strong possibility that the West has the creative process backwards!

The present-day collective consciousness is still operating as if everything starts with the physical—the domain of Content—and proceeds to flow from right to left. This shift in our thinking could be the "coming home" that spiritual disciplines throughout the ages have predicted—where we can stand grounded in the domain of spirit, more comfortable in the abstract and the immaterial, rather than standing steadfastly in the material world and discounting anything that isn't physical or mental.

Berenson's model demonstrates yet another way in which we need to think differently if we are to align ourselves with the way the universe works right now.

Choicepoint

Humanity is at a "choicepoint" in our evolution. I call it "choicepoint" because it really is a choice, no matter how much we claim reality just happens to us. If we deny that we have this choice, our attitude resembles that of the teenager who refuses to be responsible for causing anything.

I recall talking with some colleagues at a World Business Academy (WBA) meeting in the late 1980s and the word "paradigm" was being used a lot. The word's roots are tied to the academic and scientific communities, and popularized by Thomas Kuhn in his book *The Structure of Scientific Revolutions*.

Our discussion centered around the idea that we had to come up with a better word than "paradigm" because business people would never understand what it meant or use it in their own communications. It was too "highbrow," we thought at the time. It was jargon—

and like all jargon, it tended to exclude people who didn't know how to speak in that vernacular.

Well, so much for what we thought. The term is now a common word in management lexicon. One of the WBA's fellows, Michael Ray, a professor at Stanford's School of Business, started a course at the School named "New Paradigm Business." He later compiled an anthology for the WBA entitled *The New Paradigm in Business*. As Ray writes in the book's Introduction, "...the word paradigm came to mean the fundamental assumptions about the nature of the world..." He described a paradigm shift in science as "when the old set of assumptions no longer holds true, and a small band of scientists develops a new paradigm that everyone recognizes and applies, until yet another change seems necessary again."

An interesting take on paradigm shifts has been attributed to one of the world's most prolific writers—Arthur C. Clarke. The author of dozens of books, both fiction and non-fiction, this man inspired satellite development with his writings in the mid-1940s! His book *2001: A Space Odyssey* has become a modern day classic film, thanks to his collaboration with Stanley Kubrick. Clarke addresses the process of a paradigm shift when he said that any revolutionary idea goes through three stages of reaction. The first reaction is that the idea is impossible. The next stage is where people see the idea as possible but not worth doing. The final stage is when everyone claims that they thought it was a good idea all along.

I find this simple explanation very accurate in everyday life, in little matters as well as huge ones, such as the Copernican Revolution or the century it took for people to understand that the world wasn't flat after all.

Consciousness and Reality

In the fall of 1999, Russell shared some of his more recent insights about consciousness and how it refuses to be explained by contemporary science. Rather than trying to define consciousness in terms of the material world, he says, "we should be developing a new worldview in which consciousness is a fundamental component of reality." He goes on to say that the key ingredients for this paradigm shift are already in place so we need not wait for more discoveries or breakthroughs.

To facilitate mutual understanding of the term, Russell defines consciousness by its faculty, that is its capacity for inner experience, whatever the nature or degree. He then provides a wonderful example to illustrate his definition. He likens consciousness to the light shining through a projector—pure light without any content or images. Then he describes how memories, thoughts, feelings, sensations, dreams, and perceptions make up the contents or imagery that the light shines through to make images on the screen—images, shapes, and content that we focus upon.

"We know all the images on the screen are composed of this light, but we are not usually aware of the light itself; our attention is caught up in the images that appear and the stories they tell, " he writes. "In much the same way, we know we are conscious, but we are usually aware only of the many different experiences, thoughts, and feelings that appear in the mind. We are seldom aware of consciousness itself."

This content that appears in our minds is our personal reality.

Shifts Happen

A paradigm shift is difficult to explain in writing and verbally. It might be more readily grasped, at least for those who more easily take in knowledge visually, if we look at the development cycles of two paradigms in graphical terms. At the paradigm's origin, it grows out of some confusion, possible conflict, and heresy. This stage of any new paradigm is quite uncertain, such as a business start-up, a new idea being considered, or the conception stage of pregnancy. Once the paradigm becomes established it begins to grow, so the curve is drawn as rising upwards as time goes by. This stage is the equivalent of the

business growing and expanding, the idea gaining acceptance, or the birth of the baby and its subsequent growth.

At some point along the way, after some period of time and accompanying growth, the old paradigm begins to lose steam. Continuing with my comparisons, the business starts losing sales, the idea starts losing agreement or the "baby" grows old and begins to lose its vitality. Someone, somewhere could be just beginning something new as this old paradigm's straight-arrow growth begins to drop off, ever so slowly. So while the growing company's sales begin to slide (or possibly even before this time), another entrepreneur somewhere is creating a new business. As the idea starts losing credibility, another idea is being generated that might replace the older, more

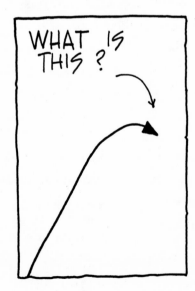

established one. A new baby is being conceived as the older one is beginning to age and lose vitality.

These cycles are the way nature works. Like trees and bushes whose leaves die and fall in the autumn and are replaced with new growth in the spring, life and death are simultaneously going on in the same place at the same time.

In their book *Breakpoint and Beyond: Mastering the Future Today*, George Land and Beth Jarman describe the three phases of growth. The first is what they call "Exploring and Inventing the Pattern." The second phase is "Extending and Improving." The third is "Integrating the New and Different" and includes the new generation of another cycle, where the old paradigm is losing credibility and the new one is still being created. They make a brilliant comparison with the way Nature works. About this third phase, they write:

> To continue growth, the original pattern must be broken, rearranged, and then restructured. The new configuration must include elements that were rejected in the second phase. Only by combining the new and different and what was previously excluded can the growing entity fulfill its potential.

In the drawing at the left, there is a valley or a cleavage between the dropping away of the old paradigm and the rising of the new one. In this cleavage lies great uncertainty. A deciduous tree in the winter may appear dead to the uneducated eye. Similarly, the old paradigm is failing and the new one hasn't established credibility yet. During this period of time, things are chaotic, crazy-making, and confusing.

I have come to appreciate the chaos and craziness since these are signs that the old beliefs and traditions are indeed failing us and that the new paradigm—one that may be far better-suited to a future of possibility—is closer to being born.

This is the time we are enduring right now. We are caught in this gap. The old paradigm is failing us and we are trying to hold onto to it—as if our very lives depended upon it. And, we can't yet see anything to replace it because the new one isn't "visible" yet, not having arrived in the mainstream nor having widespread acceptance. The only people who are comfortable with this situation are those who understand this process and are working toward bringing the new paradigm into existence.

Thus, the more people who understand this phenomenon, who understand how the old paradigm must die for the new one to be born, who understand how the old needs to be released so we can embrace the new, the more readily the new paradigm will gain acceptance, credibility, and support. This will allow us to evolve—to make this paradigm shift—to the next level as a species.

This shift in paradigms—which is presently underway—is from a mindset that has been promoted by our fixation on the hard sciences. This mindset believes we are separate beings, like gears in the machinery, individual parts of the world first and members of a "whole" second. We are shifting to a mindset that is the reverse perspective whereby we see ourselves as connected—members of the whole first and *then* as individuals or parts secondly. This reversal of perspective could be summed up as shifting from parts-to-the-whole to a perspective of whole-to-the-parts, which explicitly recognizes our interconnectedness with all other people and Nature and God.

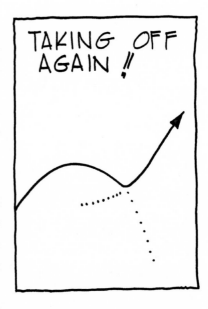

Not surprisingly, this reversal of perspective is similar to Berenson's revelations that the West has been going about everything backwards.

Fields of Possibility

In 1989, as if to prove that paradigm shifts do happen in modern times, the Berlin Wall came down. It was sudden and unanticipated. It was not organized. No one thing led to its fall. The time came for the wall to come down and it did. No one planned it. No one predicted it. The East German soldiers who stood there bedazzled did not fire their guns as they might have a day or two before. There was a "field of possibility" that existed that day, when mass legitimacy for the Wall's existence evaporated, when large numbers of people stopped allowing the Berlin Wall to be a serious part of their reality.

This was consciousness in action. One day there was a mindset that reinforced the old reality without allowing for the possibility of a new reality. The next day a new unspoken consensus mindset sprung forth, embracing the possibility and questioning why the old reality had been tolerated for so long. In the minds of so many people, the old reality lost all claims to legitimacy and was no longer acceptable.

It all happened in a "field," not unlike a magnetic field, where sufficient numbers of people shifted their thinking and, presto! The old reality was gone; a new reality was now "real."

That is how many transformations happen. That is how paradigm shifts can occur. Shifts may take time—like the century or so it took for popular opinion to change from a belief that the Earth was flat to the present-day "reality." Shifts can also happen in hours, like the collapse of the Berlin Wall, or in minutes or even seconds.

Former *Look* magazine editor and author George Leonard is a pioneer in the human potential movement. In fact, he and Esalen founder Michael Murphy are credited with naming the movement back in the 1960s. Pointing to the real potential we all possess, Leonard writes, "Each of us contains, and transcends, every form of matter that has come together since time began...Our ultimate creative capacity is, for all practical purposes, infinite."

In an article for the August—November 1999 *Institute of Noetic Sciences Review*, Leonard writes, "We stand at the vanguard, so far as we know, of the universe's journey of adventure and discovery....With a heritage and a potential such as this, how can any one of us spend a life in short-term thought and action allied with mindless consumerism?"

He goes on to say that "awareness of a problem is the first step in solving it... From this awareness can come an understanding that simply by having been born on this rare and exquisite planet we have already won the equivalent of countless lotteries...that each of us is an infinitely valuable entity, unique in the entire known universe, some-how one with nature, the stars, and the divine spirit; and that the waste of the life we are given stands as the ultimate tragedy."

Leonard's words inspire greater human aspiration, allowing us to hold higher visions for what's possible. Paradigm shifts do happen. So why can't we allow them, endorse them, invite them rather than fight them and resist? Largely, we do this because we don't understand what the new reality will be like. And, we fear what we don't know. And, we're attached to what we think we do know.

New Leadership

As we begin to understand the new reality and learn how to work with it, there will be a need for a new form of leadership. Not only will the demographics of our leaders change, but the mindsets beneath the personalities will be quite different. The term "thought leader" is a relatively recent phrase in our lexicon as ideas gain greater and greater prominence in these days of faster pace, increased "busy-ness," and growing competition. Competition is growing, not only for businesses but also for people's attention and loyalties as they are being over-whelmed with the explosion of available information. Authors are most prominent among this new breed of leader and many of them are academics. Philosophers are also seen as thought leaders, as they advocate differing priorities, values, and principles.

An example of a new leader who comes to mind is Czech Republic President Vaclav Havel, a man who rose to international prominence when he assumed office, yet his roots were in the arts, not in politics or government.

People in traditional positions which we associate with leaders, such as politicians, clergy, and even CEOs seem to rely upon thought leaders for the content of their ideals, frequently subscribing to this or that economist, philosopher, author, or professor.

Many of these thought leaders have been calling for a "new leadership." However, few of them mean replacing old leaders with different ones. This is the popular and conventional way of hearing the phrase, based upon the history of revolutions or coups and elections where people at the top of the power hierarchy are replaced by others who will hopefully do a better job.

The kind of leadership being called for by many of today's thought leaders is not a replacement of the person, but rather a replacement of the mindsets that have predominated throughout the Industrial Age and permeated the Information Age. These "old" mindsets still remain firmly entrenched in the minds of most of our leaders whether they be in government, education, business or religion.

This new leadership incorporates a transcendent perspective along with a systems view of how to deal with the complex problems of today. This new leadership also incorporates personal responsibility, so that each and every person who sees a corrective step to be taken rises and assumes responsibility. Position and titles are no longer the only requirement for leadership.

In 1997, I was invited to present a keynote address to an international business symposium in Hungary. My comments were subsequently published in early 1998 in a special edition of the British journal—*World Futures*—under the title "New Leaders for a New Future: The New Business Cosmology."

In my talk I told the audience, primarily Hungarians who were wrestling with how they were going to deal with capitalism after two generations of Soviet-enforced socialism, that I saw an incredible opportunity for them in this conundrum. I suggested that they could become the creators of a whole new "third way" that was neither capitalism nor socialism. But, it would take an entirely different form of leadership. Then I asked, "How can we become new leaders? Let us look at our assumptions—especially our unconscious assumptions. This takes great personal rigor since discovering what we don't know can be quite elusive. It requires great commitment and a willingness to see oneself naked, as it were."

I went on to say, "Here is a question about our assumptions: Is profit the purpose of a business? Many have come to believe this to be true. One of the U.S. economists—Milton Friedman—helped perpetuate this belief in the 1970s. However, as another American author Warren Bennis has so eloquently stated, "Believing the purpose of business is to make money is like saying the purpose of the human body is to keep blood flowing." Profit is essential, but not the sole reason for a company existing. There are social needs to be fulfilled by the organization, rather than it being merely a leech on the body of society, keeping itself and its owners alive at the expense of the host."

Abdication of responsibility ends with this new leadership. Parents no longer abdicate responsibility for their children's education to the school system. Citizens no longer abdicate responsibility for their communities to elected officials or government employees. They assume their rightful place as employers of these servants of the citizenry. People don't abdicate the responsibility for their health to the medical system, which has degenerated in many cases to merely treating symptoms instead of creating good health.

This abdication of responsibility grew out of society's 20th Century fascination with delegation, another product of the Industrial Age as we strove to make our systems more efficient. But, as some business people realize, delegation is not the same as abdication. Delegation requires a continuing interest accompanied by a capacity to jump in whenever there is the slightest hint of deviation from the desired outcome. That's true responsibility—or an ability to respond appropriately. Many parents in industrialized societies forgot this with their children's education, and abdicated. The children's education was now the responsibility of the teachers and the school systems. Many citizens forgot this with their governments.

As a result of this abdication of responsibility, citizens started to blame the people and the systems who were supposed to be educating the children and running the government. Finger-pointing and finding fault took the place of accepting responsibility for choices made by parents and citizens.

The new leaders who are needed for this next evolutionary shift are a responsible citizenry, responsible parents and responsible consumer base rather than a society of abdicators. These people will have strong self-awareness, having examined those previously unconscious parts of themselves, and will be differentiated and aware people who are in touch with their personal inner power.

The Power of Taking a Stand

I was told once that nothing meaningful ever happens until someone takes a stand. I know that my life changed very dramatically one day in 1985 when I took a stand on a personal issue between myself and another person. It had to do with walking tall for my own self-respect after many years of repeated cycles where I compromised myself in order to please another.

In my professional life, particularly in my work on new leadership—the transformative type of leadership I mention above, I learned that all true leaders take their "place in the universe" and stand tall for their role, their responsibility, their choice in that stance.

One of the people I most admire in the world is a woman named Lynne Twist. Lynne is a living example of someone who has clearly taken her stand in the world. She is a founding executive for The Hunger Project and serves on several boards, including the Institute of Noetic Sciences, the Fetzer Institute and the State of the World Forum—an annual event originated by the Gorbachev Foundation in 1995. In a 1999 article for *Yes! A Journal of Positive Futures*, she writes about the power of taking a stand:

> Over two thousand years ago, the mathematician Archimedes said, "Give me a place to stand, and I'll move the world." Taking a stand is a way of living and being that draws on a place within yourself that is at the very heart of who you are. When you take a stand, you find your place

in the universe, and you have the capacity to move the world.

What a powerful statement! So, let that sink in for a moment.

Lynne goes on to say, "Stand-takers have lived in every era of history. Many of them never held public office, but they changed history through the sheer power, integrity, and authenticity of who they became as a result of the stand they took....When you have taken a stand with your life, you see the world as the remarkable, unlimited, boundless possibility that it is. And people see themselves through your eyes in new ways; they become more authentic in your presence because they know you see them for who they really are."

She quotes Buckminster Fuller who once said, "When you discover the truth, it is always beautiful, and beautiful for everyone with no one left out." This is also true of taking a stand.

Lynne makes a distinction—the difference between taking a position and taking a stand. She explains that:

> Taking a *position* does not create an environment of inclusiveness and tolerance; instead, it creates even greater levels of entrenchment, often by insisting that for me to be right, you must be wrong.
>
> Taking a *stand* does not preclude you from taking a position. One needs to take a position from time to time to get things done or to make a point. But when a stand is taken it inspires everyone. It elevates the quality of the dialogue and engenders integrity, alignment, and deep trust.

She summarizes the enormous power available in taking a stand, which can "shape a person's life and actions and give them access to profound truths that can empower the emergence of new paradigms and a shift in the course of history."

A shift in the course of history! Just imagine what power people have to influence the way the world turns out simply by taking a stand about how it is to be.

CHAPTER FOUR

THE ROLE OF BUSINESS

If one could compare our present-day global society to a train, business might be compared to the locomotive pulling the rest of the cars along the track. If the business community could be likened to the locomotive, then economics could be the metaphorical equivalent to the fuel used by the locomotive to pull the train. That's how powerful our present day economic systems, particularly capitalism, have become in these turbulent times.

Given that the most influential institutions in the world are industrialized commercial enterprises and the rest of the developing world is striving to emulate them, Western business is now the de-facto leader of all global society. The modern corporation is presently influencing billions of people, affecting their values and priorities. It's called "progress" in the West and people around the world are lining up to "catch up" with this standard. Despite being dressed in this respectable gown of progress, this influence is insidious.

With such power to influence comes responsibility. Stewardship goes with the territory.

Social Responsibility

Former U.N. leader Muller writes, "Since business was the first to globalize itself worldwide, far beyond governments, and since corporations are now for all practical purpose ruling the world, we should give them the opportunity, even request them to assess their full responsibility for the future of all humanity, all living species and of all the Earth and prove to us the validity of their claim that the free market can do it all."

Businesses that do not accept responsibility for the impact they have in the world—not just in their local communities or headquarter countries—are actively promoting the first option. This is the resigned future. They are counting on the status quo continuing, with consumers remaining asleep.

Business leaders who cannot or will not examine their stewardship responsibility might find that as the world becomes more enlightened and less resigned about the possibilities for the future, more discerning and less obsessive in its buying patterns, and more holistic and less egocentric in its lifestyle, the marketplace will change drastically. As the global society gradually realizes that there is a second option and that a future of possibility can be created, business' customer base will be forever changed. When humanity elects to wake up and proactively embrace this social transformation, these inflexible companies will find themselves in the same fix as the dinosaurs, facing extinction in a world that is no longer hospitable for them.

As I wrote in the 1998 *World Futures* article:

> More and more visionary business people are becoming aware that the honeymoon with the Industrial Age is over. The past several hundred years have been quite a ride, but these more thoughtful visionaries are beginning to see the price the world is paying for industrialization, driven mostly by the West. It is as if the party was terrific, but the party is now over and we are beginning to feel the after-affects. Like a "hangover" of sorts, after excessive indulgence.

Over the years, I have interviewed about eighty leaders from around the world and edited hundreds of essays, written by some of the world's best visionary thinkers. They all agree on two conclusions:

1. Old ways don't work anymore; and

2. Even if they did, something elementally human has been missing for some time.

My vision for a better future is not at all inconsistent with a healthy vibrant business climate. My vision is not about business abandoning its charter to provide innovative and necessary products and services to a free marketplace. It isn't about businesses becoming charities. It *is* about business becoming a true partner with the rest of society in creating a compassionate and sustainable world for everyone.

In their 1999 book, *The Long Boom*, Peter Schwartz, Peter Leyden and Joel Hyatt propose an opportunity for all people in the world. Schwartz, a pioneer in scenario planning with Shell who subsequently founded a California think tank (Global Business Network), Leyden, former editor of *Wired* magazine and Hyatt, a Stanford Business School professor teamed up to advocate their version of this global choice for a better future. And they are adamant about the choice factor—stressing that the "long boom" is not inevitable. They write:

> No other age ever possessed the tools or the knowledge to do what we can do today....This is no ordinary opportunity. Only occasionally in the great sweep of history is there an opportunity like the one before us now.

> The Long Boom is not a prediction...It is meant to inspire people with a vision of what's possible...We have a historic opportunity that, if seized, can bring unprecedented benefits, but we must rise to the occasion and act. We must choose to create a better future. It won't come without us.

On this point, I agree with Schwartz and his colleagues, particularly on the need for a choice here and now and the real possibility of a better future. However, I disagree when it comes to the process of getting there. They believe we can achieve this better future through technology and economic growth and they do not mention the shift in consciousness that I believe to be essential for getting to the better future. I have less faith in "The Long Boom formula."

The Harman Legacy

Willis Harman passed on a couple of years ago, but many of us who knew him continue working under his influence and inspiration—a part of his legacy. Before he left, he wrote several books, among them *Global Mind Change* that was originally published in 1988, with a revised second edition published in 1998. In this book—my personal favorite—he describes the incredible potential of business in bringing about this historic transformation. He writes:

> If there is anything at all to the proposition that a fundamental transformation is already underway, we should see signs in the business community. For one thing, business is all-pervasive in modern society and reflects any major change in any portion of it. Moreover, business makes it its business to be sensitive to changes in its environment, and to respond to them promptly. The modern business corporation is probably the most adaptive institution humankind has ever devised.

> Leaders in world business are the first true planetary citizens. They have worldwide capability and responsibility; their domains transcend national boundaries. Their decisions affect not just economies, but societies; not just the direct concerns of business, but world problems of poverty, environment, and security. Up to now there has been no adequate guiding ethic. Although these executives and their organizations comprise a worldwide economic network, binding the planet together in a common fate, there has been within that network no tradition of and no institutionalization of a philosophy capable of wisely guiding its shaping force.

> The economic activities of the world business system have been a contributing element in the world macro-problem. But by the same token, world business will be a key actor in the ultimate resolution of the macro-problem. It crosses national boundaries with much more ease than do politi-

cal institutions, and the business corporation is a far more flexible and adaptive organization than the bureaucratic structures of governments and international public-sector institutions.

Said another way, we can bring forth a very different possible future by playing a different game than we've been playing.

I am a man who played one game for many years and then saw that there was another game I'd much rather be playing. I had to give up my image as a cowboy entrepreneur, but the game I'm playing now is like major league ball. Greater skills are required, greater consciousness is needed, and the stakes are much higher.

New Economics

The economic system that business relies upon has fueled this global crisis and a transformation of this system is necessary for us to take advantage of the opportunity being presented. The two most prevalent economic systems for the past century have been capitalism and communism/socialism, or the so-called free market economy and the central, planned economy. Both are based on materialism. One appears to have failed—socialism—and the other—capitalism—appears to be failing most of the population of the world and is in need of some serious change or transformation.

In 1993, shortly before he died, Deming's book *The New Economics* was published. In this book he makes a case for the necessity of leadership in bringing about the transformation of business if it is "to successfully respond to the myriad changes that shake the world." He goes on to say, "Transformation into a new style of management is required. The route to take is what I call profound knowledge— knowledge for leadership of transformation. Transformation is not automatic. It must be learned; it must be led."

Harman had a refreshing perspective on economics, the "fuel" that business uses to operate everyday. In *Global Mind Change*, he examined the separatedness resulting from the heavy emphasis on the scientific worldview and looked forward to a more connected society. He writes, "With the rise of capitalism the economy has become separate from, and dominant over, the rest of society. An outlook that has come to be termed "deep ecology" goes beyond the contemporary scientific framework to a subtle awareness of the oneness of all life, the interdependence of its multifold manifestations, and the irrepressibility of its tendencies toward evolution and transformation."

He then addresses the spiritual aspect of this transformation and writes, "There are today multifold signs of a respiritualization of Western society, with emphasis on self-realization, transcendent meaning, and inner growth leading to wisdom and compassion…. One of the most striking changes in the past two decades has been the extent to which people are awakening and feeling empowered to take responsibility for their own lives and for changing society as necessary. This has happened in both industrialized and developing countries."

I mentioned this phenomenon of respiritualization in my chapter in the 1998 anthology *The New Bottom Line: Bringing Heart & Soul to Business*. My chapter was titled "Spirit and Work: Can Business and Consciousness Co-Exist?" and I wrote:

> Much of this phenomenon can be attributed to a reaction to the overbearing influence of the Industrial Age, which resulted in the mechanistic, reductionistic thinking that has dominated the West (and parts of the East) for more than a century. We have come to think that the whole is the sum of the parts, that value exists in what is external to us, that rationality and the mind are the ultimate "justifiers of our actions."
>
> This kind of thinking has been valuable for technological advances and creating wealth for a relatively few people, but it has not done much for maintaining a sense of community with each other, for developing sustainable lifestyles that allow our environment to continue supporting us, or for enriching our inner lives, our intrinsic sense of self identification.

Fortunately, there is a movement of sorts within the business community—a movement that is still largely underground. It is a revolution in the brewing stages, like the "invisible revolution" I mentioned earlier which has not yet become obvious. One of the bits of evidence for this movement is the numbers of books that have been published in recent years that address spiritual values and spirituality in business.

Spiritual Renaissance in Business

As *The New Bottom Line* was being prepared for publication, we received a number of pre-publication endorsements, including one from Stephen Covey, author of the incredibly successful *7 Habits of Highly Effective People* and all its descendants. In his endorsement, Covey wrote, "This anthology effectively captures a spiritual renaissance taking place in the business world today..."

Even Peter Drucker, author of numerous business books and considered by many to be the father of management theory, addresses our need to explicitly acknowledge our spirituality. He writes that "man is not just a biological and psychological being but also a spiritual being..."

This spiritual renaissance has included many progressive business books in the past decade. The rise of popularity in these books prompted a reaction from consultant Tom Peters in 1994. Peters sees religion and spirituality as being very similar and thus argues against there being any place for spirituality in the workplace. A "First Amendment freak" by his own definition, Peters confuses these two words as so many do in our society. So, let me take a moment to distinguish between them.

Spirituality vs Religion

One of the most widely debated topics among proponents of transformation is the distinction between spirituality and religion. Many people shy away from any mention of the "S-word" because of their childhood experiences with religion. But the confusion is certainly not limited to those who've been burned or disillusioned in the past. So the field is quite muddy, even among the sophisticated.

Spirituality serves as a context for interconnectedness with those parts of ourselves that are not necessarily material or physical. It is formless. It contains no specific content or dogma. It allows for a direct relationship with the Divine through one's personal experience.

Religion is based on specific concepts or form in which spirituality is viewed. It contains beliefs, rules, structure and, very often, tradition. It takes many forms, usually based upon the teachings of an enlightened being such as a prophet or someone else who is seen as having a very special relationship with the Divine.

Religion and spirituality exist in two different—sometimes separate and sometimes overlapping—domains, which is one reason why people find it so difficult to discuss them together. Spirituality is abstract, personal, and experiential. Religion has a specific form, is objective, and has defined content. Berenson says that "religions are forms whose purpose or objective is to access the spiritual."

The Dalai Lama explains the difference between religion and spirituality in his book *Ethics for a New Millennium.* He defines religion as "claims to salvation of one faith or another." He states that spirituality is expressed through certain "qualities of the human spirit— such as love and compassion, patience, tolerance, forgiveness, contentment, a sense of responsibility, a sense of harmony."

Further, he writes, "Religion is something we can perhaps do without. What we can't do without are those basic spiritual qualities."

Interface, Inc.

Another example of this spiritual renaissance in business is that of Ray Anderson, founder and CEO of the billion dollar carpet maker Interface, Inc. Anderson had what he called an "epiphany" after reading a book by Paul Hawken, *The Ecology of Commerce.* Hawken, himself a businessman and the co-founder of Smith-Hawken, the gardening tool retailer and catalogue company, also wrote a book that became a popular PBS television series "Growing a Business."

When I interviewed Anderson for an article in *The New Leaders* in 1996, I learned just how dependent the carpet industry is on petroleum-based chemicals. As a result of his epiphany, Anderson committed his company to becoming sustainable within a very short time window, after recognizing just how much impact his company was having on the Earth. He subsequently wrote a book entitled *Mid-Course Correction: Toward A Sustainable Enterprise: The Interface Model.* In it he writes:

> My company's technologies and those of every other company I know of anywhere, in their present forms, are plundering the earth. This cannot go on and on and on.

> However, is anyone accusing me? No! No one but me. I stand convicted by me, myself, alone, and not by anyone else, as a plunderer of the earth. But no, *not* by our civilization's definition: by our civilization's definition, I am a captain of industry. In the eyes of many people, I'm a kind of modern day hero, an entrepreneur who founded a company that provides 7,000 people with jobs that support them, many of their spouses, and more than 12,000 children—altogether some 25,000 people. Those people depend on those factories that consumed those materials! Anyway, hasn't Interface paid for every pound of material it has bought and processed? Doesn't the market govern?

Anderson then goes on to show how taxpayers actually pick up the expense of military protection of Middle East oil, weather damage due to global warming, and medical costs for treating disease caused by toxic emissions. He goes on:

> Do you see how the revered market system of the first industrial revolution allows companies like mine to shift those costs to others, to *externalize* those costs, even to future generations?

> In other words, the market, in its pricing of exchange value without regard to cost or use value, is, at the very least, opportunistic and permissive, if not dishonest. It

will allow the externalization of any cost that an unwary, uncaring, or gullible public will permit to be externalized—*caveat emptor* in a perverse sort of way. My God! Am I a thief, too?

Yes! By definition that I believe will come into use during the *next industrial revolution* [a phrase originated by Hawken and architect Bill McDonough]...

Anderson's ground-breaking public candor demonstrates that business people have a conscience and can recognize the negative impact they are having once their attention is focused on the realities. In Anderson's case, all it took was reading a book.

A Closer Look at Capitalism

Hawken was included in an interview conducted by *Yes! The Journal for Positive Futures* in its Summer 1999 issue on the future of the corporation. He and David Korten, author of *When Corporations Rule the World* and former Ford Foundation executive, were asked to discuss the prospects for change under the present economic model of capitalism. They exchanged their thoughts in the featured article entitled "Corporate Futures." Here are portions of just one exchange between them:

Hawken: ...I agree with David that financial capitalism, the capitalism that is in place and practiced, is bizarre and cancerous...Capitalism arose from industrialism without any particular framework or values. It was sometimes given lofty virtues by observers, much as conservatives do to this day, but social and environmental values were never intrinsic. Capitalism simply emerged. No one said, wouldn't it be cool to have a juggernaut economy of unprecedented productive capacity that destroys the capacity of every living system on Earth, where over 90 percent of the world's wealth would be concentrated in the hands of 2 percent of the people, and the other 98 percent wouldn't mind because they were being anesthetized by shopping or the eventual prospect of having more material goods...

Korten: ...So far as I can see a mindful market economy has no need for institutions created for the sole purpose of enriching the already wealthy and concentrating economic power without democratic accountability. The problems arise from a combination of size, ownership, and accountability and are best resolved by replacing the global publicly-traded, limited liability corporation with human scale, stakeholder-owner enterprises that are accountable to the communities in which they are located. Nor is there any place in such an economy for financial speculation...

Hawken: ...It is frustrating to see the juggernaut of corporatism continue to concentrate ownership in the media, energy, transportation, publishing, apparel, and so much more and not feel like power is being swept away and sequestered in to the hands of the few. Although the rate of corporate change is accelerating now, sometimes you have to bite your lip when you see what passes for change. Is an institution making a legitimate effort to transform its culture and direction or are they just standing on the first rung of the ladder for a better view?

....We are talking about some very entrenched and highly reinforced paradigms that have been drilled into the head of every MBA in America, not to mention overseas. It isn't easy to change. Even CEOs who do understand sustainability extraordinarily well....say that they have a difficult time being understood by other CEOs. Those barriers permeate the organization, not just top management. Nevertheless, it is the executive suite that poses the greatest barrier....I agree with David's view that we are goal-less. What are the goals of corporate America?

Hawken's question hits home. Beyond making a profit, what are the goals of the modern corporation? Getting beyond the rallying rhetoric of vision statements about serving their customers, better quality, and all that how do these legal entities whose life is unlimited continue their self-serving ways when the public can revoke their charter at any time when the public trust is breached? It's due to the public's apathy, ignorance, and complicity in keeping the system going.

Korten's concern over speculation is another major challenge in changing our ways. Former *The New York Times* business editor Joel Kurztman estimates that the speculative or financial economy in the currency markets—mostly electronic exchanges that have nothing to do with the trade and goods economy in which most of us participate—to be more than 16 times bigger than what most us think of as "the economy."

In his 1993 book *The Death of Money*, Kurtzman states that, compared to this monster speculative economy, "the world's real transactions are small indeed. The financial economy, which used to be the dog, is now the tail," he writes. "As a consequence," he continues, "speculation holds far more sway over each nation's economic livelihood than we generally give it credit for."

This explains, at least in part, why the economic system as a whole is the most insidious and often pernicious system facing the industrialized peoples of the world. Speculation doesn't breed partners or investors. It only promotes short-term holdings and loyalty to nothing other than the dollar.

The Robber Baron Model

The real estate investment firm which I co-founded in the late 1970s specialized in purchasing income properties, holding them for a short term of four to seven years, making any obvious improvements that would enhance resale value and then disposing of them. Everyone earned lots of money. But, aside from increasing investor wealth, was there any other value we created for the neighborhoods, the community, or the world? I'd have to say not much.

Now that I look back, I can see that we were professional speculators. On behalf of the partnerships with our investors, we acquired property without any intention to be landlords for the long haul.

I call this model for business people doing good in the world the "robber baron model" whereby an entrepreneur or investor makes a fortune in some industry that capitalizes on the exploitation of people and natural resources and then sets up a trust or foundation to give *some* of that money away to worthy causes. That way, they are seen as benefactors for their charitable work while any negative aspect of their commercial enterprise activity is largely ignored. Many of the early millionaires in the U.S. followed this formula.

While my partners and I were making lots of money, I was also keenly aware of the growing stress on the world over the nuclear arms race. After eight years of making money on a grand scale, I started a small foundation so that I could put some of my energies into contributing to the improvement of the world—something beyond making a few hundred people a few million more dollars.

Then, I began wondering why a person couldn't have a business that actually did something good for the world and its people—making a profit *at* doing good rather than making a profit *then* doing some good with the spare change that was left over after a lavish lifestyle was assured. Despite these wonderings, I was still following the "robber baron model" of making as much money as I could, as quickly as I could, in order that I might focus on making a difference in the world.

I expected that my partners and I would be able to cut back considerably in the near future and then I'd be able to put even more time into the work of my foundation, which was going to promote systems thinking and holistic attitudes so as to lessen the tensions and mistrust between the superpowers. As it worked out, my partners and I divorced and parted company in mid-1980s, the decade of excesses, which eventually put me into the full-time business of working toward a better world.

The 1980s Relived

The so-called "Decade of Greed"—the 1980s—saw many mergers and acquisitions among the larger corporations while Wall Street was intently focused on improving stock value in the short run, making huge sums for a few people. This was also the decade of the junk bond and savings and loan scandals. MBA students were expecting to be millionaires within five years of graduation so long as they went into investment banking during this time.

Twenty years later, there's a similar dynamic going on in Silicon Valley according to a number of financial mavens, including Michael Lewis, author of *Liar's Poker* and *The New, New Thing*. Interviewed in *San Francisco Magazine* in late 1999, Lewis told the interviewer that "Earnings out West were putting '80s Wall Street to shame." After noticing that Solomon Brothers had moved to California from New York, Lewis also moved West and realized that "money, not the latest software, was the new story to be told." According to the magazine, Lewis saw "that Silicon Valley, resembling nothing so much as arbitrage-infested, currency-swapping nutso-crazo Wall Street—a place consumed by the art of the deal rather than the creation of new technology—is the latest chapter in the perennial American romance with success."

The Consumption/Production Cycle

Cousins to the speculative economic system are the production and consumption systems. Consumption is necessary in order to have the production levels we insist upon, and vice versa. One feeds the other. Like the alcoholic who relies on the co-dependent person or system to enable his or her drinking habit, we all need to agree that consumption is good so we can go to work and produce all that stuff, so we have more to consume, so we produce more, and so forth.

There's no doubt that many of the large, legal, private-sector entities that have evolved in the free market system—chiefly multinational publicly-held corporations—have become socially insensitive, environmentally cruel, and are doing their best to make a few people very rich at the expense of the vast and growing majority of the Earth's population. You could say that they are the biggest culprits at perpetu-

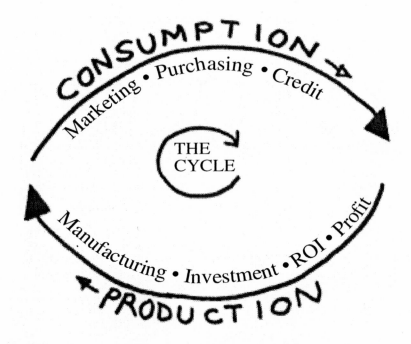

ating the growing gap between the Earth's "have's" and the "have not's"- a potentially dangerous situation for all of us. But while the corporations are the identified culprits, like the drunk is in an alcoholic system, there are more elements to this system that keep it going.

Futurist Didsbury addresses the hedonistic nature of our society which is "captivated by the siren call of instantaneous gratification." He writes, "...there is no call of personal service or sacrifice for the general good but rather there is established an unassailable tyranny...the concentration of interest on and the pursuit of everything for the here and now."

He describes our "sensate society" in which production and consumption collaborate "to create catalogues of endless wants." He goes on to say that this system "serves as a form of operant conditioning in the arousal and perpetuation of insatiable desires." He then ponders a challenging scenario in quoting E.J. Mishan, author of *On Making the Future Safe for Mankind*:

> There is no need to enter the debate on the efficacy of commercial advertising in [molding] people's tastes. Speaking only of the broad social repercussions of commercial advertising, one can hardly deny that it does appear to have succeeded wonderfully in one of its aims— that of making people discontented with what they already won. Indeed it is hard to imagine anything that would throw the American economy into greater disarray than a religious conversion that made most Americans perfectly contented with their material lot.

Due to my pro-bono work as a trustee for The Club of Budapest Foundation in Hungary, I have become better-informed and more observant of the struggle between ideologies in Central Europe. As people wrestle with this shaking-out process, we can see the darkest parts of capitalism—"brutal capitalism" at its worst—leaving a few people and businesses "filthy rich" while their fellow countrymen struggle for their basic survival needs. In the November 13, 1999 issue of *The Economist*, a teacher from what was formerly East Germany was quoted. "Certainly, my standard of living is higher now," he says. "More importantly, I can go where I want, say what I want, do what I want. But not everything in the GDR was bad. Maybe we couldn't buy many luxury goods, but food was cheap and no one went hungry. At least everyone had a job. And human relations were better. I needed my neighbors and they needed me. We all helped one another. Now people are more isolated. We often don't even say hello to each other any more."

Changing Capitalism

Economist Lester Thurow, former dean of Sloan Management School at MIT and author of *The Zero-Sum Society*, addresses the challenges facing capitalism today. In his 1996 book, *The Future of Capitalism*, he examines the often idolized economic system, now that its competitors—fascism, socialism and communism—are all but gone as competitive factors. He writes, "The eternal verities of capitalism—growth, full employment, financial stability, rising real wages—

seem to be vanishing just as the enemies of capitalism vanish. Something within capitalism has changed to be causing these results. Something has to be changed to alter these unacceptable results if capitalism is to survive."

In exploring how this might be achieved, Thurow describes how systems resist change, shedding some light on the difficulty of changing any complex system, much less the most dominating system in the world today. He asks, "How does a system that believes it takes competition to make the firms within capitalism efficient, adapt to a changing environment and maintain its efficiency if the system of capitalism itself has no competition? Perhaps with all of its competitors driven off the economic playing fields, capitalism has lost its ability to adapt to new circumstances?" He goes on to say:

> Those who govern the existing system, no matter how left-wing and revolutionary their political ideologies, are social conservatives. The system has chosen them to rule and therefore it must be the "right" system. Without any outside or inside threats to the existing system, all changes lower the probabilities that they will continue to rule in the future. Since they know that they govern by virtue of today's rules, they instinctively oppose change—different people might govern if the rules were different.

Thurow touches upon one of the basic laws of systems theory: Regardless of what it was originally designed to do, any system will adapt a primary agenda—to resist anything that it perceives as a threat to its existence. In other words, a system will defend itself first, even if it means abandoning its stated purpose.

Systems Thinking

Systems thinking is undoubtedly a more appropriate way for us to engage modern life for it is consistent with the complexity of the way things are these days. Simple cause-effect thinking is adequate for dealing with very simple systems. If you wish to slide a brick across a table, you apply pressure at one end and it will move along the direction you are pushing. We can all recall those experiments in high school physics class involving pressure, mass, velocity, and force.

A few generations ago, our work lives were similarly simple. Farm life was very simple. As part of a farming family, there were your family members, the chores, and the crops to deal with. This was still a fairly simple system, a system that rarely changed. The people in your life tended to remain in your life as long as you and they lived. The generation preceding you lived on the farm and the one following you was expected to live there also.

The Industrial Age changed all that. All of the systems with which we interact these days are significantly more complex than a century ago. Everything moves more quickly now. The pace is dizzying compared to our grandparent's time. Change has become an everyday occurrence, not a rare phenomenon. Our culture has become enormously diverse as well as incredibly more complex. Organizational life is a product of the past half-century and has become extremely complex in those few decades. The definitions of "family" and "home" have been completely rewritten since the turn of the century, adding even more dimensions to the complex world we live in today.

In the world of business, when one thinks about complex systems and engaging them, MIT Sloan Management School's Peter Senge comes to mind quickly. A relative late-comer to the scene of thought leaders, Senge has become one of the leading business consultants and global authorities on large-scale organizational change since his book—*The Fifth Discipline*—was published in 1990. Mentored by Sloan Professor Emeritus Jay Forrester, he also co-created a course offered by a consulting affiliate, Innovation Associates, which has since become part of the international consultancy Arthur D. Little. The course is Leadership and Mastery, which I attended in the early 1980s and in which I first learned about systems theory.

While there are many pioneers in the field of system thinking—from the biological, therapeutic, and health perspectives—Senge has found himself firmly entrenched as the leading expert in this field from the organizational perspective. It's safe to conclude that he introduced the concepts of systems thinking and its cousin the "learning organization" to business people on a global scale that exceeded any previous proponents.

Senge and his colleagues at MIT's Society for Organizational Learning look at the world through the lens of dynamic living systems—seeing the interconnectedness and interdependence of all the elements of the system and the dynamics among those parts. This perspective is quite different from the conventional mechanistic way of looking at relationships. He calls systems thinking a "sensibility" that allows us to experience the subtle nature and balance of complex systems. In *The Fifth Discipline*, he writes:

> Today, systems thinking is needed more than ever because we are becoming overwhelmed by complexity. Perhaps for the first time in history, humankind has the capacity to create far more information than anyone can absorb, to foster far greater interdependency than anyone can manage, and to accelerate change faster than anyone's ability to keep pace. Certainly the scale of complexity is without precedent.
>
> Complexity can easily undermine confidence and responsibility...Systems thinking is the antidote to this sense of helplessness than many feel as we enter the "age of interdependence." ....systems thinking offers a language that begins by restructuring how we think.

Senge portrays a rainstorm as an example of a complex system that can only be understood by contemplating the whole system, not any specific pattern or part. He writes, "Business and other human endeavors are also systems. They, too, are bound by invisible fabrics of interrelated actions that often take years to fully play out their effects on each other. Since we are part of that lacework ourselves, it's doubly hard to see the whole pattern of change. Instead, we tend to focus on snapshots of isolated parts of the system, and wonder why our deepest problems never seem to get solved."

One of my first learnings about systems was how most people and organizations focus on the apparent problem when trying to get a system to improve—to do what was intended for it in the first place. This approach is an example of cause-effect thinking. Almost always, attention to this obvious problem is wasted, since the other elements of the system—the parts, the relationships among those parts, time delays, and other elements—need to be included and understood as best they can. Usually, there is what Senge calls a "leverage point"—a place in the system that may not appear to be involved in the dysfunction at all—where attention can be better spent in improving the performance and understanding the system.

Consciousness in Business

In 1999, I wrote an article entitled "The Conscious Organization" anticipating a forthcoming anthology I had compiled with the same title. In this article I put forth a vision of what was possible for an organization that would be viable and thrive in a post-transformation world. I wrote:

> Humanistic psychologist Abraham Maslow's Hierarchy of Needs declares that self-actualization is a state sought by all human beings once we have satisfied the more basic needs of survival, gratification and belonging.
>
> It seems quite reasonable that as we humans continue to evolve and become more conscious beings there will be a concurrent need for our organizations to follow suit. As people continue on their path of self-actualization, the enterprises, institutions and companies where human beings come together to produce results will need to change dramatically or die.

I didn't mean to alarm business leaders with such an ultimatum but I do deeply feel a sense of urgency that may require some dire warnings if we are to get the attention of the people who can make change happen.

When people 'wake "up" and come together to work, forming an organization, it stands to reason that such an organization needs to accommodate people who are awake. As I wrote, "This suggests the genesis of the "conscious organization"—not an end-state where every worker has been certified "enlightened" and each and every element of the company, or division or bureau, or agency, or institution is spotlessly cleaned of any residual unconsciousness. The Conscious Organization is one that continually examines itself, committed to becoming as conscious as it can. In other words, it has very low tolerance for unconsciousness. It possesses the collective will to be vigilant, the collective commitment to continuous evolution, and the collective courage to act." I continued:

> Once this Conscious Organization, or anyone involved with it, recognizes a quality, procedure, or other element of its culture which is not conscious, a rallying cry goes out and the organization's resources are marshaled toward "cleaning up" that area and making it more conscious.

Sound Utopian? Seems like "New Age claptrap," you say. Well one of the most respected business thought leaders in the West, Britain's Charles Handy, has been getting more and more insistent upon big -time change in how business operates with each book he writes. He was involved in the founding of the London Business School, where he also served on the faculty after an executive stint with Shell Oil. He's written six books, including *The Age of Unreason*, a book I was given by a friend a decade ago. I've since had the privilege to get to know Handy and his wife Elizabeth, a portrait photographer. Handy has become one of the world's foremost business philosophers and is widely recognized as Britain's "top-tier" management writer.

In his 1998 book, *The Hungry Spirit*, Handy writes about a world beyond traditional capitalism. He states, "Capitalism needs to be reinterpreted to make it decent, and companies, which are key institutions of capitalism, need to be rethought. Education should be redesigned to prepare us all for more personal responsibility. Government needs to return responsibility to the people. Only then can we feel that life and society is ours to shape. Were that to happen, our values could dictate the way things worked, rather than the other way around."

Handy has become more outspoken with age and with his growing acceptance as a global business philosopher—one of the world's few Western management elders like Warren Bennis and Peter Drucker. People who identify with his words are growing in numbers, thus providing him with greater license to challenge the status quo. About America's cowboy entrepreneurs, he writes:

> Ross Perot is wrong. Untrammeled individualism corrupts a nation. It leads to an emphasis on rights, with no regard to duties or responsibilities.

Later in the book, Handy goes on to say that "Left to themselves, things do not necessarily work out for the best. Laissez-faire is value free. No one is responsible for anyone else. That is improper selfishness and can self-destruct. We need something better. Capitalism as an idea includes social capital as well as economic capitalism. One without the other will not work for long."

One of Handy's concepts that I find absolutely tantalizing is his "Doctrine of Enough." He sometimes refers to this a "decent sufficiency" as well as "elegant sufficiency" —two other endearing terms I find equally engaging. He elaborates here:

> It is, of course, easy to say that enough is enough when you quite clearly already have enough. The problem for most people is getting to that stage. A society which adopts the doctrine of enough has to make it a priority to ensure that everyone has a real chance of being able to reach their personal level of enough, so that they can move on....The philosophy of enough cannot be imposed on a society. It is a matter of norms, not laws.

Handy goes on, thinking aloud as it were, but letting his readers know that they can begin to think differently, for this is the only way out of the trap we have created for ourselves. Like the monkey who gets caught by the trapper because it refuses to let go of the fruit it has clenched in its hand when it reached through the tiny hole in the cage, we need to let go of our grasping in order to be free.

Another business leader who has seen the writing on the wall is Visa International founder Dee Hock. When I first read the short excerpt below, I was absolutely flabbergasted to learn that it was written by a CEO of a multinational organization the size of Visa. An obvious thought leader among the successful business ranks, Hock states:

> We are at that very point in time when a 400-year old age is rattling in its death bed and another is struggling to be born—a shifting of culture, science, society and institutions enormously greater than the world has ever experienced. Ahead lies the possibility of the regeneration of individuality, liberty, community and ethics such as the world has never known.

Is it possible that to date there's been a sort of "conspiracy of silence" among business folks? TV producer Norman Lear was interviewed for one of my anthologies in 1994—*Leadership in a New Era.* He shares that he had an insight about business people. He remarks that, based on feedback he's received, "business people weren't ready to step forward and declare publicly the experience they've held privately."

A New Business Cosmology

If capitalism "simply emerged" without any explicit values as Hawken stated earlier, it has certainly leaned on Adam Smith's 250-year-old idea that market forces will take care of things and the "invisible hand" will balance self-interest with the interests of the whole. With all due respect to the "father of capitalism," Smith's words are outdated in today's world. However, fundamentalist capitalists still cheer to his metaphor, many of them using his ideas as justification for taking their self-interest to some brutal extremes.

Another outdated standard that's been adopted by mainstream business, particularly in the U.S., is a much more recent proclamation from Milton Friedman, a member of the 1968 Nixon committee of economic advisors and one of the most influential economists in modern times. Friedman—who later received the Nobel Prize for economics —opined that a company's primary loyalty should be to its owners—that business's responsibility was solely to its stockholders.

Directors and chief executives were quick to pick up Friedman's 1970 decree—treating it with all the reverence of a papal decree from Rome—and have been reciting it ever since as justification for all kinds of financial shenanigans. The repercussions from this pronouncement from such a credible figure have been far-reaching. Contrary to Smith's vision of a market economy and his outdated words due to the passage of time, Friedman's relatively recent decree was totally contrary to a healthy global society and quite the opposite of life-affirming for people and Nature.

For business to be in concert with the Age of Consciousness—to be in step with the new music of the emerging era—it needs an explicit "cosmology," a way of being in the world so that it knows its role, its responsibilities, and the expectations that the rest of our society has for it. At present, as Hawken infers, there is no explicit cosmology. Nor is there any real explicit philosophy, other than echoing the decrees of Smith and Friedman.

While most dictionaries define the word cosmology as having to do with the nature of the universe, I'm using it to define the essential philosophy of how business relates to the world in a universal sense, such as the larger context or ultimate role or destiny it has in the cosmos. This inquiry goes far deeper than the narrow view promulgated by advocates of Smith's invisible hand and Friedman's decree. What I'm asking is a very similar question that many people – people like me—are asking at the individual level. The question for me was "what role do I really play in the universe?" or "why am I here?"

It is time for business to ask this question of itself. What is the ultimate role for business in the world? How can business be constructive in the evolution of humankind? After all, like human beings, business has hardly reached its apex as a contributor to the overall evolution of humanity.

And, as Bennis reminded us earlier, making a profit is hardly the sole purpose of business. So, what is the ultimate role for business—explicitly? It needs a new cosmology.

Reactionary or Visionary Approaches to Change

Part of this new business cosmology—this new way of relating to the rest of the cosmos—involves business's approach to change. Most executives, strategists, planners, and consultants spend their time anticipating projected changes based on trends or reacting to changes going on in the present market climate. They pay enormous fees to futurists to tell them what they can expect. This approach is *reactionary*—reacting to either a perceived or an anticipated change that will impact one's business.

There is plenty of evidence that changes are happening at record rates and managers are reacting to them much like an escaped convict trying to dodge a hail of machine gun fire being sprayed in his path.

Change management has become an entire field of practice with specialists including consultants, interim managers and CEOs, and business school faculty. One of the most requested topics for keynote speakers these days is change, change management, and dealing with the difficulties of change. The rate of change is so overwhelming that trying to "manage" it is tantamount to "whitewater rafting" under extreme conditions, a euphemism coined by George Washington University professor of management Peter Vaill.

But how about the changes we *want* to make? What about envisioning a future—the way we want it rather than the way we think it's going to turn out? Why not stop *reacting* to all these incidental changes that are bombarding us and focus on *creating* a future we find preferable? What about getting on the other side of change and bringing about the changes we want rather than learning to cope with changes happening to us?

Which side of this issue is the most empowering after all?

Why stand there getting plummeted with *unauthored change* and learning defensive strategies and coping mechanisms when we can be *authors of our own futures*—our own reality? This is the new business cosmology—creating a future of our own choosing for the world rather than adapting to whatever changes come our way.

Wouldn't that be exciting?

Cosmology and Spirit

Cosmology and spirit go together. Matthew Fox, author of *The Reinvention of Work*, tells us that theologian Thomas Aquinas said that "spirit" means our capacity to relate to the totality of things and cosmology means the whole or the totality. He writes, "Bringing spirituality and cosmology together is an altogether natural process for human beings. It's living without a cosmology that's unnatural and rare."

If this is so, those of us in business have been living *unnaturally* so far.

Consciously developing a new cosmology for business will require mental rigor that may tax the minds of many career business people who are used to focusing on strategies, techniques, and models. Creating a new cosmology will force them to look at the larger picture and ask about deeper purposes that merely generate profits or increase revenues next quarter.

A Leader with No One to Lead

Before I close this chapter on the role of business, I must mention the role of the U.S. in bringing forth this new cosmology for enterprise. After all, America has been the primary driver for capitalism worldwide and bears much of the responsibility for both the positive and negative impacts this new capitalism has had on the rest of the world.

While this thinking has been percolating in the minds of many business philosophers for a decade or so now, mainstream media is just now beginning to address this issue. *U.S. News & World Report* published an editorial in its October 18, 1999 issue that addressed the widening gulf between rich and poor in the U.S. Entitled "A Nation Divided," Editor-in-Chief Mortimer Zuckerman pointed out the uneven distribution of wealth in this country. His article points out that when it comes to wealth-building, *all* of the growth from 1983 to 1997 has been for the top 20% of Americans!

That leaves 80%—four out of five households or 217 million people—taking home *less* than they did over twenty years ago.

Coincidentally, *The Economist* published an editorial within one week in which their editors looked at how "The United States bestrides the globe like a colossus." U.S. domination was the central focus of the editorial and, in particular, our country's insistence on "going it alone"—to act unilaterally without many allies and consistently putting its own interests first."

The article concludes saying that America "may be blissfully free; but it will also be alone. It will be a leader with no one to lead, in a world made unstable by its very isolation. This is sovereignty, all right. But a superpower should be bigger, and wiser, than that."

"The past is gone...The future is another matter. It is an open field of possibility."

— Howard Didsbury, Jr.,
Frontiers of the 21st Century: Prelude to the New Millennium

CHAPTER FIVE

ULTIMATE RESPONSIBILITY

All of this talk about a new business cosmology, planetary consciousness, new economic models and the other topics I've discussed here can be seen as mere platitudes if we don't address what it all means to the individual. This is where the rubber meets the road.

Everything I stated heretofore can be readily agreed-to by many of you. So, left to the human mind, these ideas are "interesting"— possibly even compelling—but they can also remain as purely idealistic, noble as they might be. Hence they stay in the domain of concept, the mental realm.

They make interesting cocktail party conversation and stimulating discourse. But that's where they can end unless we bring these conditions, challenges, and possibilities into the realm of the individual. Bring these ideas into the realm of personal reality—what they mean to you and me—makes them "actionable." They are no longer relegated to "interesting discourse" and are now part of "what does this mean to me?"

Values and Hypocrisy

How we live our lives as individuals speaks volumes for what values we hold. What we say we believe, what organizational credos we endorse, and who we associate with does not necessarily reflect who we are at our essence—as our essential Selves. These associations, endorsements, and pronouncements do reinforce the images we have of ourselves, our personas. But images of who we are and what we stand for are far different from being authentically ourSelves—fully aware, mature, and conscious beings.

Robert Rabbin, a modern day mystic who wrote *Invisible Leadership: Igniting the Soul at Work*, writes and speaks with a rare directness that I find very attractive and quite provocative. He deals with hypocrisy in much the same way when he writes:

> I never listen to anyone speak about their values. My ears slam shut and I go deaf. I'd rather watch them. The truth is we are always expressing our vales; it is nonsense to think that what we say and what we do are two separate things which must be brought into proximity...We might *think* that our real values are what we say they are, but that is a delusional conceit. Our real values are expressed in our actions, in what we do and how we do them. Our actions never contradict our values: our actions *are* our values.

"If we believe our values are what we say they are," Rabbin writes, "then we will also believe all the reasons and excuses we give about why we don't live up to them. The simple reason we don't live up to our espoused values is that they are not our actual values." He goes on:

> We don't need to refer to any papers or books or stone tablets for our values. Doing so creates unnecessary tension and anxiety which further obscures what we actually do. We act from what we are, from what is written on the tablet of our hearts. If there is some values work to be done, it is there, in our hearts. We need to change who we are from the inside out, not because someone else says we should but because we have looked into the mirror of our actual behavior, and we don't like what we see.

Rabbin's writing goes right to the point of individual responsibility—to the "heart" of the matter so to say. The hypocrisy we all hold in our hearts, the public self that all of us must own to some degree, is another of those shadowy parts of ourselves that requires illumination if we are to transform ourselves, our organizations, and our society.

Responsible Choices

One of the most popular daytime television shows in the U.S. is the Oprah Winfrey Show. In 1998, Winfrey—one of the world's wealthiest and successful women in the media and host of the show—started a closing segment at the end of her daily shows which she called "Remembering the Spirit." One of her shows featured best-selling author Gary Zukav, author of *The Seat of the Soul*, who was invited on the show after a number of years of private telephone conversations between himself and Winfrey. The show was so popular that Zukav was subsequently featured for one week in the new closing segments and then, some months later, a summary of his segments. Finally, in July of 1999, he returned to the show to discuss "responsible choices", and living with the consequences of the choices one makes in life— whether they are conscious or unconscious.

The Oprah Winfrey Show has thirty or forty million viewers, mostly women. Zukav's first appearance in 1998 resulted in a huge resurgence in sales of his nine-year old book, boosting it to Number One on *The New York Times* bestsellers list after nearly a decade of being in print.

However, the 1999 show about responsible choices was a blockbuster—at least from my perspective! Zukav and Winfrey worked brilliantly together, with the author speaking with incredible clarity, free of any jargon or empty rhetoric. The host did a magnificent job as a facilitator, so the points being made could be understood by anyone watching the show. I was so impressed that I now recommend that one-hour show for anyone who thinks the world is "treating them badly" and expresses any interest in changing their life.

Zukav's point was that we all make choices. Many of these choices may not be conscious ones so we may be unaware of some of our choices. As he told the TV audience, "If you are not aware of all the parts of your personality...those parts you're unaware of will make your choices for you...They will become your obsessions, your fixations, and your addictions."

We have a choice in how we respond to situations and we have a role in what we attract to ourselves. If we chose to believe that the world can't ever change, for example, then we will attract circumstances that reinforce that belief. During the telecast, Zukav stated, "The world of your experience will always validate your beliefs."

This is another way of saying that we create our reality, what we perceive as our reality, as seen through our perceptions, which are filtered through our beliefs, which were established by choices we made and are continuing to make.

One of Zukav's key points is that we need to accept the consequences of our choices, bringing the issue of personal responsibility for our lives into the picture. This is where the buck stops, where the finger pointing ends, and where the truth is being told. After all, if we are not responsible for our lives, who is?

In *The Seat of the Soul*, Zukav writes:

> The center of the evolutionary process is choice. It is the engine of our evolution. Each choice that you make is a choice of intention...What you choose, with each action and each thought, is an intention, a quality of consciousness that you bring to your action or your thought.

> You cannot choose intentions consciously until you become conscious of each of the different aspects of yourself...Unconscious evolution through the density of physical matter, through the experiences that are created unconsciously by unconscious intentions, has been the way of our species to now.

> Conscious evolution through responsible choice is the
> accelerated way of evolution...the conscious road to au-
> thentic empowerment.

While Zukav's writing is meant for the individual, his words have profound meaning at the organizational and societal levels as well, and I mean at the global level. Just like individuals, the marketplace has obsessions, fixations, and addictions—such as material consumerism, to name just one glaring example.

Win-Win Versus Win-Lose Worldviews

When people have chosen to believe that the world is an unfriendly place, or that people are out to get them, or any other cynical, fearful, or resigned worldview, they tend to unconsciously attract circumstances and situations that reflect their beliefs. The reality they create for themselves reinforces their belief system. These less-than-conscious viewpoints all suggest separation—that is, that each of us are separate parts without any experience of our being part of some larger more inclusive whole. With this consciousness, business people might think they have to dominate their industry or they'll be failures, or that anyone who sees them being vulnerable will take advantage of that vulnerability. They may think they have to be ruthless in all their business dealing or people will see them as "weak" and that will work to their disadvantage.

If someone holds on to an unconscious belief that the world has something against them—not everyone, just *them*—they are likely to create a trail of failures in their careers, or wins that were "miraculous" because of all the adversity they had to overcome. I know plenty of people who have attracted this kind of adversity—they were convinced the odds were against them so they might as well get credit for pulling off a "miracle" and beating the odds.

A very simplistic lens through which to view the way people with these worldviews see things is to look at them as owning a philosophy that if someone wins, someone else needs to lose. This lens is what perpetuates the paradigm that suggests that *you* have to lose if *I* want to win; that someone needs to *fail* if I *succeed* so that my success or winning comes at someone else's expense.

How about war? If you think of we humans as disconnected individuals who are each subscribing to some set of values, you could easily adapt a position that there are those of us who believe "X" and "them" who believe "Y"—they who believe quite the opposite. Therefore "they" are bad and wrong and "we" are right and good.

Another example of this mindset or worldview lies in how a person looks at world hunger. Someone who believes that the world is a collection of individual egos, separate from any sense of wholeness, might also believe that ending hunger is absolutely impossible, contrary to The Hunger Project, which sees the problem as one of distribution, not sufficiency.

One reason that I know this particular dynamic is that it was one of my personal favorites for a good part of my life. For many years, I unconsciously harbored a core belief that nothing good would ever happen to me unless I *made* it happen. This meant I believed that the universe was somewhat hostile. As a result, I selected very risky ventures when I was younger, like promoting events that the public had never heard of so they were a brand new product, and I was always under-capitalized. As I look back, I can see how much I tempted fate, almost asking for failure given my high disregard for risk in some of my ventures.

Contrarily, people who hold an attitude that the world is a friendly place, one that doesn't have any particular grudge against them personally, might find success to be far easier and treat people very differently than their more cynical counterparts.

These people live a life whereby they only win while others can also win, where their getting what they want doesn't require someone losing or not getting what they want. Their philosophy may include the experience that we are all connected, parts of a larger whole but nevertheless interconnected like family, like blood relations.

When it comes to conflicts or wars, these folks see us all as brothers and sisters—connected at a very basic level—hardly people who we want to kill or wound each other. The same goes for violence of any nature. How can a person who sees the world as a collection of interconnected souls, living in a grand experiment here on Earth, suggest anything other than the need to work out any differences, difficulties, or conflicts. What sane person, truly believing that we are all connected and interdependent, would suggest that we start shooting at each other, or shelling each other, or dropping bombs on the other?

The interconnected worldview—this new paradigm—suggests a "win-win world" versus a "win-lose world," a worldview available to every human being on Earth.

What Can One Do?

Quite often when I'm speaking to groups about this scope of such a transformation, I'm asked the "what can I do?" question. The helpless tone in which most of these questions are asked suggests that the people asking them don't think they can do much of anything at all. This helplessness has become an epidemic. Perhaps I should say that avoiding the feelings of helplessness has become an epidemic. This epidemic of rationalized impotency and the unexperienced or suppressed feelings of hopelessness lies at the core of the growing cynicism throughout our global society.

But, each human being is unique—with strengths, weaknesses, interests, and abilities that vary widely. I often wonder at the miracle of six billion people on this planet, each one being absolutely unique.

Part of my own uniqueness is that I can work, write, and speak at this larger contextual level, in an attempt to translate or simplify the knowledge being offered by so many wise people. Since many of these wise people have written or are still writing in a language that might be off-putting to a wider, popular audience outside of their peers and colleagues—I try to make it more accessible to a wider audience, putting it into a sort of "street language" for non-scholars and non-academics. That's what I do. Others work at other levels and in other ways, none better or worse than any other—just unique.

Given that we are all uniquely gifted and destined, there are an unimaginable variety of ways we can help bring forth a new paradigm. But there are also certain actions that we humans engage in every day, actions that reinforce the status quo, or the old paradigm, without our even knowing it. There are also actions that we *don't* take, acts of omission that allow things to go on as usual. So, for those who might be interested in what they can do as individuals, here are a few suggestions that you may find useful.

Stop Doing Things That Perpetuate the Old Paradigm

First of all, there are definitely activities you need to stop doing if you are doing them. Generally, I suggest that you look at whether your actions are life-affirming, nurturing, loving, and done with integrity. If they are, continue doing them. Do they compromise your sense of right and wrong, even if they might be legal? If they do, then stop them. Remember, that's how business rationalizes its impact on our society, using the law as a barometer so "if it isn't illegal it's OK." Here are some other things you can stop doing:

Stop Squandering Your Life: Living and working without maximizing satisfaction, fulfillment, joy, and spiritual growth is tantamount to squandering your time here on Earth. Stop it right now.

Stop Disconnecting: If something doesn't bring people closer together, and adds to a disconnection among them, stop doing it. If something doesn't expand people's sense of themselves but instead causes them to contract—to shrink up—then stop it.

Stop Compromising: If you are doing anything that compromises your integrity, stop it now. Immediately! Compromising our values, going along with something we know to be wrong or unjust or unethical or immoral poisons our souls. It kills us spiritually. Stop it now.

Stop Posturing: Stop putting yourself above others in order to feel better about yourself. This kind of vertical or hierarchical thinking promotes similar activity among others, which ultimately results in everyone trying to out do everyone else. I find this to be particularly popular in the U.S. where cowboy entrepreneurship has been such a big part of our culture. Standing out is how people have succeeded in the states, at least that's how it looks. Consultants posture by flaunting their past clients. Executives posture with their perks, or their salaries, or their achievements.

There's another form of posturing, which is putting yourself *below* others for any variety of reasons. This should also be stopped as it is unhealthy for everyone.

Posturing is also putting one's value or worth *outside*, making it comparable to someone else. True self worth comes from inside, from a sense of having authentic power, regardless of external factors.

I recall a conversation I was having with a young woman with whom I worked in the early 1990s. I was expressing my curiosity about the new wave of MBA graduates who didn't seem interested in learning. They rarely asked questions, I told her, seeking any insight she might offer as a recent business school graduate herself. She informed me that, by the time they had completed business school, most students had adapted a posturing style as a result of getting good grades. Whenever they engaged in class discussions, they saw their task as one of impressing everyone with what they knew. As a result, their personalities had become habitualized to spouting pseudo-wisdom rather than seeking true wisdom.

Posturing is related to another epidemic in our society—egocentricity. The world does not need any more self-centered people. The world needs people who are differentiated *and* who operate in the world in a way that is responsible for the whole. If you are behaving in an egocentric way, grow up. Accept that you have failed to mature emotionally and proceed to become a mature adult. The "what's in it for me" and the "let everyone else worry about themselves" philosophies are outmoded and won't be tolerated in the Age of Consciousness.

Stop Denial: Stop denying that you have any role in keeping dysfunctional systems in place. You do. Accept this fact and get used to it. If you work in or for a company or if you buy products of any kind, you are a part of this economic system that is so pervasive and dysfunctional. You either add to the production of goods and services or you consume them. In most cases, people do both. And who doesn't? It would be a challenge to find anyone who might have access to this book who didn't fill one of these roles. If you are part of a system, you play some role in keeping it going.

You can stop supporting any dysfunctional systems in which you are a part. The world is loaded with systems that aren't very functional. Many of them actually create more harm than good. Most of them are more concerned with maintaining themselves than doing what they were created to achieve. We are all part of many systems with which we interact each and every day—the legal system, the education system, the political system, our family systems, the economic system, our cultural or ethnic systems, and so forth. There could be hundreds that you don't even think about. If you see something going on that isn't right, and you either remain silent and/or go along with the "way things are done here," you are adding credibility and legitimacy to that system, reinforcing it every day.

Stop Lying: Lying is either stating something that isn't true, giving an opinion as a fact, or allowing someone else's lie to go unchallenged. Lying keeps old ways locked in like mortar is to bricks.

If the emperor has no clothes, it serves everyone involved to tell the truth so his nakedness can be addressed.

Stop Taking Consolations: Stop fooling yourself, taking consolations as you attempt to cope, to adjust your ideas about reality to fit with your unconscious beliefs about how the world has to be. Consolations are ways to appease our egos for a short time while we continue to postpone our ultimate destiny. Consolations may provide gratification for the time being but they can add to a self-delusion that prevents movement along one's personal growth path.

I suggest that the Western world's fixation on consumption and our obsession with having the latest model car, the highest-tech computer (even though we can only use a small portion of the features in the ones we own), and trendy fashions are mostly consolations we give ourselves as a coping mechanism. Our personalities get a boost—a temporary rush—as we take pleasure in the new acquisition, the new toy that we've purchased. But our souls know that these things are emotional sugar candy, empty of any spiritual calories that mean anything in the long term.

Stop Adolescent Behavior: You can stop any adolescent behaviors that you continue to act out. Since most of us haven't really matured into fully-functioning emotional adults, there are most certainly times when we act out our adolescence. Think about these episodes, such as saying or doing something to please your peers or get their approval. How about bending the rules, breaking traffic laws, and other little acts of rebellion against the rest of society?

Stop Degrading: Do you degrade or abuse yourself or others, not necessarily in the headline producing ways you read about in the newspapers but in more subtle ways? Do you berate yourself or others when a mistake is made? Are you hard on yourself when you forget something? Are you so self-judgmental that you curse yourself when you make a mistake? Do you do similar things to others you care for, like your spouse or your children? Remember, emotional or verbal abuse can be just as traumatic as the physical or sexual abuse that you read about, whether it's directed toward yourself or toward others.

Stop Prejudice: Are you prejudiced against any other person or group of people? Do you view differences in people's gender, color, ethnic origin, religion or any other aspect of their personality or being-ness as a basis for judging them as less-than or subordinate to you? Do you work with others who share your prejudiced view? Are you aware of the enormous synergy available when there are diverse perspectives represented in a work team, a neighborhood, or any other grouping of peoples?

If you are prejudiced, either privately or publicly, do what you need to do so you can see the value of diversity. Why? Because that's the way things are and the privileged group in the Western mindset— white, middle-aged men—are a small minority of our global society.

As a white American and middle-aged man, I recall a very tough insight I had in 1998. I was attending a workshop on the subjugation of women in the world and it hit me just how privileged I was, merely by my gender, race, and nationality. I saw my complicity in the subjuga-tion of women by taking that privilege for granted. It was a difficult insight to allow in, but I shall remain changed by it forever.

Stop the Conspiracy of Silence: Another thing you can stop doing is remaining silent when something is going on in your presence that you disagree with. The biggest epidemics in the world today are "conspiracies of silence" where activities are perpetuated because no one objects to them. Silence can be tremendously empowering. Re-member the high school bully? Bullies rely on silence; they count on people remaining quiet about whatever is going on. The silence gives them power over others. It allows them to maintain the fear people have of them.

I'm reminded of the "Abilene Paradox" parable (popularized by Jerry Harvey in his 1988 management book of the same title) where a group of people took a long drive into Abilene, New Mexico during the

This unattributed story was sent to me by a colleague who found it on the Internet. I claim no ownership of it and have no way of knowing its author. But, it does emphasize the point made by the Abilene Paradox *and I am very grateful to whomever created it:*

Put 5 apes in a room. Hang a banana from the ceiling and place a ladder underneath the banana. The banana is only reachable by climbing the ladder. Have it set up so any time an ape starts to climb the ladder, the whole room is sprayed with ice cold water. In a short time, all the apes will learn not to climb the ladder.

Now... take one ape out and replace him with another one (ape 6). Then disable the sprayer. The new ape will start to climb the ladder and will be attacked unmercifully by the other 4 apes. He will have no idea why he was attacked.

Replace another of the original apes with a new one and the same thing will happen, with ape 6 doing the most hitting. Continue this pattern until all the original apes have been replaced. Now all of the apes will stay off the ladder, attacking any ape that attempts to, and have absolutely no idea why they are doing it.

This is how company policy and culture is formed.

heat of one summer day. It was very hot and quite dusty. Everyone was very uncomfortable, crowded into a car without air conditioning. They stayed for a while, then returned. At one point someone stated that they really had a miserable time. Another person agreed. Then another. Finally, someone asked whose idea was it to go to Abilene. As it turned out, no one had actually suggested they go at all! The idea grew from something said idly during a conversation, which got built upon as the gossip spread and next thing everyone knew—the whole group was crowding into a very warm car to take a ride that no one wanted to take.

There are many "Abilene Paradoxes" in our lives, made possible because someone didn't ask, "why are we doing this?" Or "who wants to go?" Or "what is the purpose here?" The conspiracy of silence resulted in this entire group of people having a miserable time doing something no one wanted to do in the first place! This can be easily compared to how our world is progressing today.

Stop Averting: A few years ago, I began walking every day. Since I live in a city, I come across many people in my daily jaunts. I have noticed how most people refuse to make eye contact with me, despite the fact that we are passing within inches of each other on the sidewalks. When I look at them and they've been looking at me, they immediately avert their eyes, usually downward, but often toward some imagined item of interest. If they sense that I'm looking at them, they keep their eyes averted. This aversion, this refusal to connect with another human being, goes on with nearly everyone I pass during my walks. Are we so afraid of each other that we cannot greet one another with a friendly "hello?"

I see this aversion as symbolic of how we are averting our consciousness about many things. You can stop doing this! Engage other people. You don't need to ask them out on a date, or even like them, or even say anything, but acknowledge their existence. After all, they are your fellow human beings. They are not objects and they are not invisible.

As I mentioned earlier, to some degree, we all have conspired to act in these various ways. No one organized us, or declared that this was the way to be, so the conspiracy has grown silently. Using the example of the averted gaze by someone on the sidewalk, it is easy to understand that if people consistently fail to acknowledge you as you pass each other you might feel hurt, unimportant, or insignificant. So you develop your own protection mechanism. Rather than feeling that way, you simply comply and do the same thing. That way you don't need to feel anything. Of course, you do pay a price, as does the other person: you are both cutting that human connection. Then, later in the evening when you watch the evening news on TV, you wonder why people treat each other so badly.

Look and see if you are part of a mass conspiracy to *separate* ourselves and, if you are, stop it. You may not be able to end the conspiracy but you can stop participating in it. You can stop giving it legitimacy.

Stop Hanging Out With Cynics: If many of the people you spend time with are cynical about the world and the future in general, back away and spend less time with them. The social system we find ourselves in has enormous influence on us and how we think, so separating from people who are negative, resigned and cynical is truly an act of self-love.

Stop Ignoring the Shadows: While it may seem easier to ignore or pretend you don't see certain things in your life, your family and your organization, you do pay a dear price for ignoring these dysfunctional aspects in your relationships. You cannot have a conscious life while you continue the pretense that you are "in the dark" about certain negative aspects of who you are, how you relate to others and the conditions you allow to persist by keeping your head in the sand.

Stop Participating So Fully in the Production/Consumption Cycle: The Production/Consumption system continues to spiral more and more out-of-control, like an airplane in a spin toward earth. By being an active part of this cycle, you are contributing to society's addiction just as surely as if you were giving cheap wine to the homeless alcoholics on the streets. By being part of the systems that either manufacture goods that aren't really necessary or acquiring products which aren't essential, or doing *both* (as most of us are), you are a part of the problem—like it or not. If you can't stop doing it entirely, at least cut back.

Stop Being Hypocritical: Stop telling people that you stand for certain things that you don't. Stop espousing values that you don't live by. Stop lying to yourself if you are doing it. "Own" your values and end the hypocrisy that you put out in your life.

Stop Making Irresponsible Choices: End any patterns of unconscious decision-making and choices that are adding to the dysfunctionality of your life, your relationships, your work and the world. If you are attracting negative realities into your life, recognize that there's some part of yourself that isn't aware of what it is doing and choices it is making.

Start Doing Things That Facilitate the Emergence of the New Paradigm

Just as there are many actions and beliefs that keep the old paradigm alive that one can stop perpetuating, one can do many things to facilitate the arrival of the new. These actions and behaviors *connect*—they bring people closer together as members of the human family. Here are just a few suggestions for things you can do to connect.

Start Telling the Truth: Speak that which is true and accurate from your experience. This includes interrupting and correcting those who are lying or putting forth inaccurate information or information that does not match your experience; otherwise, your silence can be taken for approval or agreement, thus furthering the lies and misconceptions.

Start Feeling: Being in touch with one's emotions is the single greatest means to having a spiritual life and becoming a more conscious human being. Men have more to learn here than do women, but all of us have a ways to go in this department. Despite growing acceptance of showing one's feelings in public in some parts of the world, feelings are still largely suppressed worldwide. In addition, most people aren't even clear as to what a feeling is. You can hear this in their conversations, when they say, "I feel that you are mistaken" which is clearly a *thought* being described as a *feeling*.

Using the word "feel" to convey a thought does not make it an emotion. It is still a thought, whatever you call it. Thoughts evaluate.

Feelings don't. Its that simple. The widespread use of phrases such as these makes it apparent that we have a ways to go in understanding our emotions.

Start Dialogue: Genuine dialogue has been displaced by discussion and argument, even if politely disguised and socialized. Having a dialogue with someone or a group entails silence as much as sound—something you seldom witness in group or couple interaction. If people are speaking to let others know that they are better informed, single and available, looking for investors or any other agenda, there's no dialogue. Real dialogue consists of people coming together to further the purpose of coming together. In dialogue, one remains silent and listens if one doesn't have anything to further learning. The silence is valued. One speaks when one is moved to speak. Manipulation of others—to get a date, to become admired, to ingratiate oneself for any reason—has no place in dialogue. And, silence is valued. After all, if something needs to be said, it also needs to be listened to.

Dialogue is only possible when all of the parties agree that the exchange shall be a dialogue rather than a debate, discussion, or a social conversation (like about the weather).

Start Being Yourself: Your spiritual destiny calls for you to be absolutely and authentically yourself. Like Gary Zukav points out in his book *The Seat of the Soul*, the authentic self in not the personality. When you are in your personality, your social persona or image is being projected, much like an actor playing a role onstage. Your authentic self is the true you, your real Self, the part of you that has a unique destiny and purpose in the world. Sound like a big deal? You bet it is! So, with the possibility of recognizing your purpose in life and fulfilling your destiny for this lifetime, why waste one more second living from your personality and pretending you are anything other than who you are, really, down deep at the core?

Start Dreaming: If you haven't encouraged yourSelf to dream big dreams, start now. If you already dream big, then dream bigger. I'm not talking about fantasies—made up ideal situations that we never expect will happen to us. I'm defining dreams as creating a field of possibility where their realization is not unanticipated despite their grand nature. Dreams and visions set a generative context for miracles to happen. Intention plays a big part here too. Expectancy—not expectations— also plays a big part. Expectancy is a field, minus the specific form of expectations. After all, for miracles to happen specific expectations may be too limiting. Expectancy allows for things to exceed our expectations in big ways.

Start Thinking Systemically: If you don't know General Systems Theory, learn it. If you aren't sure if you are a systems thinker, make sure you are. As I stated earlier, thinking systemically allows you to see many of the dynamics in all the relationships in your life—personal, business, and organizational. It gives you the means of thinking that fits with the complex life we live these days.

Start Thinking Global: Most of us concern ourselves with our immediate relationships—family, co-workers, and friends—with little attention on anything outside of our circle. We may pay attention to the news and the events reported there but we do little with that information other than adding it to our inventory for social conversation at cocktail parties and water cooler chit chat. To be a responsible world citizen one needs to have a greater awareness of Nature, other nations, and global situations. Feeling compassion for people in other parts of the world, being aware of developing countries, and paying attention to different cultures are all ways of expanding your thinking so you can think globally. I've always found Buckminster Fuller's idea of "Spaceship Earth" to be a good metaphor, pointing out the need for humans to rely upon each other if we are to survive, as if we are all on board a spaceship in outer space. We'd think very differently if we knew the survival of each one of us was reliant on the survival of all of us—the entire "crew" of Spaceship Earth. And survival is essential if we are to evolve to a higher plane of consciousness.

Start Growing in Consciousness: If you aren't already doing it, start making your personal growth—your spiritual, emotional, and psychological development—a top priority for your life. I'm often saddened when I see so many people who appear resigned to their lot in life, struggling through their years on Earth, where feeling hopeless has become a way of life and resignation and cynicism are their antidotes. You can always change yourself. You can always change how you respond to circumstances and how you see the world. It is never too late or too early to start growing.

Start Growing Up: Move into being a true adult—emotionally, spiritually, and mentally. Embrace genuine maturity and model adult behavior and thinking.

Start Respecting Life: Begin to appreciate and respect everything alive. That not only includes the lovable beings like dolphins and eagles and babies, but all of the people of the world. It also includes yourSelf, your personality, your persona, and all those parts of yourSelf that you are unaware of, including your shadowy side. When you realize that you aren't living a life of respecting everything alive, do whatever you need to do to achieve that respect.

Start Obeying the Law, or Change It: I've noticed that many of us who consider ourselves to be "people of integrity" manage to find some areas where we don't comply with our social codes for getting along together. Some exceed speed limits when they're driving. Some fudge on their income tax returns. Others walk across the red light at intersections. If you disobey the laws of our society, you are out of integrity. You are breaking the law. Stop cheating. The alternative is to change the laws if you don't agree with them.

Start Finding Your Passion: Passion feeds your soul. Passion provides you with the juice, the fuel to follow your dreams, to proceed toward your personal destiny. If you don't feel passion for your life or your work, begin looking and praying for it immediately. You are not here on Earth to live a life of mundane drudgery or resigned toil or unenthusiastic existence.

Start Hanging Out With Optimists: Begin spending time with people who reflect positive attitudes about the future, people and the world. I'm not suggesting that you surround yourself with delusional dreamers who have no sense of the reality in which they live, but there are plenty of folks who are grounded in reality who also possess a very healthy, positive outlook about things. Start spending more time with these people.

Start Looking for the Shadows in Your Life: Shine the light of consciousness into the "dark spots" in your life, your relationships and your work or organization. These pockets of unconsciousness, after all, steal our vitality, suck out our lifeforce and contribute to the collective unconsciousness that allows for so much suffering in the world—our own and that of others. Seek out the darkness with enthusiasm rather than dread, knowing that a more conscious life means greater happiness, contentment, joy and aliveness.

Start Reducing Your Participation in the Production/Consumption Cycle: By remaining passively involved in this system, you are adding legitimacy to the dysfunctionality of the whole global addiction to unnecessary and destructive consumption. If you bring awareness to each of your choices to produce and consume (or both), you will automatically reduce your participation.

Start Being Authentic: The more authentic we all become, the more consciousness we bring into the world. Hypocrisy diminishes as we become more "real" and genuine, living from a place of authentic empowerment—not artificial external power but true personal power.

Start Making Responsible Choices: Bring your awareness to all your decisions and choices you are making and review past choices you have made, assessing them for consciousness. Change those choices that you've made unconsciously. If you are confused by why you've made some of the choices you have, seek consciousness in those areas by shining some "light" into those darkened spots.

SOME THINGS TO STOP DOING	SOME THINGS TO START DOING
1. Squandering your life	1. Telling the truth
2. Disconnecting	2. Feeling
3. Compromising	3. Dialogue
4. Posturing	4. Being yourself
5. Denial	5. Dreaming
6. Lying	6. Thinking systemically
7. Taking consolations	7. Thinking globally
8. Adolescent behavior	8. Growing in consciousness
9. Degrading	9. Growing Up
10. Prejudice	10. Respecting life
11. Silently conspiring	11. Obeying the law (or change it)
12. Averting	12. Finding your passion
13. Hanging out with cynics	13. Hanging out with optimists
14. Ignoring the shadows	14. Looking for the shadows
15. Participating so fully in the production/consumption cycle	15. Reducing your participation in the production/consumption cycle
16. Being hypocritical	16. Being authentic
17. Making irresponsible choices	17. Making responsible choices
	18. Looking for the opportunities in crisis
	19. Maturing
	20. Practicing creative tension
	21. Taking stands

Start Looking for the Opportunities in Crisis: Recognize that while the dangers are important to acknowledge in any crisis, there are opportunities to grow, to learn and to evolve to new personal, relational, organizational and societal levels.

Start Maturing: With the goal of becoming wise and fully adult, assess your maturity level. Examine the maturity level of the activities in which you engage, the people with whom you associate and the systems in which you function. If our species is still at an adolescent level and still evolving, then it figures that those of us who make up society are also evolving and becoming more and more mature. Put awareness on this process and look at ways you can create a level of maturity for yourself that serves you and the world.

Start Practicing Creative Tension: Learn to live in the tension between what your vision is for your life and the world and the way you see reality right now. Master being in this tension and holding your vision without feeling the need to lessen or eliminate the tension.

Start Taking Stands: Take a stand that can move the universe! Stand up for what you believe in. Put yourself on the line and stand tall for those values and priorities, those visions and dreams that you have for yourself, your family and friends, and your world.

Finding Passion or Letting Passion Find You

An impassioned life is an examined one. Self-examination alone, of course, isn't sufficient. One needs to take some action as the result of what was discovered in the examination. I know plenty of people who probe themselves constantly, digging for every last bit of emotional garbage from the past. They find a wound here, an affront there. It becomes a lifelong process of sweeping every nook and cranny of their psychic closet in an attempt to get it white-glove clean. And, of course, it never gets that clean!

This is not the action I am speaking of. There comes a time when enough of the sweeping—healings from the past—has been done. Like when you sweep the remnants of dirt into a dustpan—you know how you can never quite get all of the dirt? There's always some small residue that you just have to ignore and move on. That's how it is with the examined life.

There comes a time when you know there's been enough sweeping and now's the time to start creating the future and stop dwelling on past healings. And, examinations of one's life need to happen regularly, not just once or even twice, but as needed to keep the spark alive. Sometimes we find our passion early in life. Sometimes we find it in our later years. Sometimes, it finds us! Examining your life is an ongoing process that stays with you so long as you remain committed to your spiritual growth.

Once you find this passion (or it finds you), evasive as it may be, there are countless ways you can apply it so you make a difference in the world.

" As the proportion of people reaching higher states of consciousness increases, this inertia will decrease, and at the same time a supportive momentum in the new direction will start building up."

— Peter Russell, author,
The Global Brain

CHAPTER SIX

A NEW AGENDA FOR BUSINESS

One project for which I felt a lot of passion was a relatively recent one in which I worked with several dozen others, and it could have worldwide influence in improving the state of the world.

In the early part of 1999, I was part of a group of visionary business people who put forth a public resolution—a sort of credo—for doing business in the this century. The idea behind this resolution was to provide a place where anyone from any part of the world who was interested in seeing business change the way it operated could add their name to this resolution for all to see, thus creating credibility and legitimacy for the values and priorities contained in the document.

It was a kind of modern-day version of posting a public petition in the town square for all the citizenry to read and sign if they supported it. The Internet, being the current equivalent of the world's bulletin board, was the posting place. We all recognized that this means of posting the resolution would eliminate a good number of people from being able to sign it, since having access to the World Wide Web was a technical requirement. But, we felt that the people we'd be appealing to would, for the most part, possess this technical ability, so we went ahead with our plans to post it in cyberspace.

There were forty-two of us from sixteen countries who were involved in drafting the original resolution, critiquing it, and putting our names on it as original "co-signers"—a term we created to describe anyone who eventually signed on and agreed with the tenets covered in the resolution.

We named the document "The 21st Century Agenda for Business" and described it in a subtitle as "A Global Resolution for New Corporate Values and Priorities." Since then it has become known simply as the "Agenda."

While the full text of the Agenda contains a number of tenets, the vision it contains is quite simple. Within the Agenda's resolution is the following paragraph:

> We the people who have co-signed below agree with the tenets included herein and commit to the following vision: *a world in which the global business community serves society in ways that are life-affirming, sustainable, humanistic and responsible for positively influencing the future evolution of humanity.*

In addition to the words used in this document (which actually consists of two parts—a "preamble" and a "resolution") we believed that it would be very important that no one person or group of persons were identified any differently than any other person who signed this resolution. We also believed that it was equally important for the success of the project that no one person or organization be identified as the designated author or sponsor of the resolution and that it not *belong* to anyone. As a result, there is no copyright to the Agenda. It belongs to the world.

The idea was to post this resolution on its own homepage, so people could read the resolution and "sign" it while they were there. This would eliminate any email forwarding or chain letter-type activity and allow for all the co-signers' names to be listed in one place for the world to see.

To maintain the anonymity of the original group of co-signers, we decided that the names of co-signers would be listed alphabetically, so there would be no hierarchy among the co-signers. We also agreed that we'd ask co-signers to list themselves by name, city, state and country, and include a few words describing their business credentials so visitors to the Agenda could get some idea as to the geographic diversity and the credibility of the existing co-signers.

The rationale here was that if the Agenda was going to have any impact in influencing the status quo and impressing today's business leaders with the agreement generated by this resolution, the co-signers needed to be seen as "credible" in the eyes of the people we wanted to influence. In that older paradigm, this means title, achievement, success, and rank.

The original group of us then invited some colleagues and friends to a beta-test site where the Agenda was posted temporarily so we could test the signing-on process. The temporary site was up for one full week and the invitees tried signing on, uncovering some minor technical problems that were corrected within another week. By then, we had 225 co-signers and we were ready to go "public" with our baby.

In mid-July 1999, the Agenda was publicly posted on its own homepage. I host it on my Web site, without any linkages or back buttons making it impossible for anyone to go to any pages other than those associated with the Agenda. There's no hidden or covert purpose in having it hosted on my site. It is simply a matter of economics.

We included a sample letter that people could use to invite their friends and colleagues to see it, a registration form to sign on and instructions for people to link their sites with the Agenda if they so chose. It was programmed so that people could see their name added to the growing list after they signed on.

Next, everyone who had signed on was encouraged to tell their friends, family members, and colleagues – that is: promote the hell out of it! Every co-signer who joins the Agenda's growing list of supporters agrees to promote it to their networks in addition to adhering to the values and priorities outlined in the resolution.

The full text of the Agenda is included in Appendix A of this book, so you may read it at your leisure and carry it with you in this book. However, to become a co-signer you need to access the Agenda's URL, which is http:// www.the-agenda.net.

A reminder: the Agenda's homepage is entirely automated and not overseen or managed by anyone.

"Go to http://www.the-agenda.net"

I encourage you to go there and presuming that you agree with the tenets of the resolution, join those of us from around the world who have agreed with these values and priorities. As the list grows, and every additional co-signer helps, credibility for these principles grows so that at some point the mainstream business community notices the acceptance these tenets have received and may start paying more attention. Then the Agenda will have achieved its objective—a new cosmology for the business world.

CHAPTER SEVEN

COMING HOME

As Albert Einstein said many years ago, we can't solve our problems with the same consciousness—the same thinking, logic or ideas—that created them in the first place. He told us that our thinking was outmoded over half a century ago! As the decades have rolled by, we humans continue to apply old thinking to new problems. We haven't heeded Einstein's advice even in the face of growing evidence that he was correct.

I have adapted his observation somewhat, stating that we can't solve 21st Century problems with 20th Century thinking. As our society has become bigger and more complex, so must our thinking—our consciousness.

Unless we change the way we've been thinking (and subsequently act), the future we are headed for will contain more of what we have now—continued loss of community, growing cynicism, and increased alienation and incivility. These trends will continue to the point of eventual irreversibility. This future is inevitable if we do nothing to change the direction in which we are headed.

The *other* future is one we can create...an ability we possess for the *first time in human history*. This desired future is possible if we change our thinking. I don't mean to change what we think *about*—the content of our thoughts. I'm talking about changing the very basis for *how* we think—what academics call our "worldview" or how we see the world and our relationship to it and everyone else in it, including Nature and the cosmos.

After all, we don't really think this is the final stage of our evolution do we? Can any thinking individual honestly believe that we have reached our full potential as human beings?

The human race is *in* a race between these two possible futures— the "future of inevitability" that will surely result if humans refuse to accept our Divine inheritance, our birthright of consciousness —and the "future of possibility", a cocreative partnership we form with the Divine, accepting our destiny as conscious and spiritual beings in physical form.

Our Human Destiny

Our Divine inheritance—to grow and evolve in all dimensions without limit, without restraint—is our human birthright. Higher and higher states of consciousness are available to us, as long as we continue to be willing to grow, to live in concert with all the forces, immaterial as well as material, the non-physical as well as the physical. After all, we are parts of the whole—elements of the Divine—with wonderful opportunities for synergy as a result of this consciously acknowledged relationship. Synergy provides far more than the sum of the individual parts and synergy with the Divine holds limitless possibilities, blessed with vision, joy, learning, love, fulfillment, and authenticity.

But embracing this destiny requires giving up our old thinking—thinking that is filled with limitation, fear, narrow-mindedness, cynicism, the past, and pretense. That's the thinking that got us this far in our evolution. However—and this may be the main point of this entire treatise—it is now time to let that thinking go and embrace a new worldview and new mindsets, a process similar to the shift in conventional thinking that needed to take place as a result of Copernicus and his revelations about the planets a couple hundred years ago. In many ways, people had to switch off centuries of knowing reality as it had been. They had to embrace a whole new way of seeing reality, a way that was backwards from what they had believed to be "true" before.

Creating a sustainable and positive future will come easier if the world's most influential institutions recognize this possibility. The most dominant and influential institutions these days are most assuredly the commercial enterprise, the modern corporation. Like it or not, business is leading the rest of society. Economics drives *everything* these days as undeveloped countries try to catch up with the West and *be just like us.* If the rest of the world succeeds in doing everything "just like us," we will most certainly deliver the inevitable future.

Businesses that keep their wagons hitched to this inevitable future might be in for a rude awakening in the coming years. On the other hand, those people and organizations who become more responsible for the future and lead us in creating the "future of possibility" may soar—lighting the way to a truly transformed world.

I am convinced that a preferred future—the future of possibility we all would prefer to the inevitable future—lies just outside of our present reality—and within our reach if we change the way we think about what is possible.

The Conscious Organization

Businesses that join in this creative process—this ultimate experience of co-creation—will be hitching their wagons to unimaginable realities for us all! And, who wouldn't want to be part of such an experience—creating a future loaded with possibilities? As a veteran businessman, I'm quite confident that as soon as the business community sees the possibility—not as some New Age fantasy but as an achievable reality—it will jump in with both feet and assume the lead with great enthusiasm.

So, how do all these wonderful ideas get implemented? How does a business in today's chaotic economic climate become conscious?

Remember Berenson's Four Domains of Reality?

Possibility and pragmatics live in two separate domains or realms. The domain of possibility lives in a more generative, contextual, and abstract realm. As the "context of contexts"—the place where the origins of our experience and subsequent thinking are born—this domain does not include forms and content. They live in different domains—ones far more familiar to those of us raised in the West or in most industrialized nations.

Contrarily, the abstract, contextual and generative domain— also known as the spiritual domain—is far less easily discussed. Conversations in this domain are generally uncomfortable and unfamiliar, especially in business circles, and thus are often avoided.

Within this domain or field of possibility—the generative domain—lies the creative energy that subsequently generates the processes that result in the form and content with which we are all so familiar. This domain is where vision resides. This is the domain where desire lives. This is the place where the spirit of service hangs out. This is the domain that ultimately generates the answers people are seeking. Strategies and practices and policies that originate out of the other domains, while locking out the generative domain of context, are doomed to failure—like rearranging the deck chairs on the Titanic while it continues on its way toward the iceberg.

Some of the activities that many are doing to "save the planet" deal with form and content. Recycling, participative management, and cleaner manufacturing technologies are all helpful, but not in themselves paradigm-changers. They extend the viability of the old paradigm, adding to its usefulness for another relative moment or two, considering the timeline for the evolution of humanity. But these activities will not, by themselves, transform the system or change the paradigm.

I'm reminded of another Berenson concept here. He talks about people who do the best they can so as to make their condition in life more tolerable. So, those who believe that the world is against them and life is difficult, and the universe is an unkind and unloving place, may acquire lots of possessions, or have wonderful lovers, or surround themselves with plenty of friends. Activities motivated by a desire to "make the most" of the situation under the circumstances, could be consolations or little offsets to make them feel better about the state of things. He compares taking these sorts of short-term consolations to "decorating one's jail cell"—a phrase that has stuck with me over the years.

Embracing Context

Organizations that console themselves by adapting—accepting changes in form and content without examining the underlying context for their existence and purpose—will die slow deaths. They will become extinct because they are out of step with evolutionary forces.

In order to get where we want to go in our companies, we need to honor context without passing it off as "ungrounded" or "irrational" or "not-businesslike" or any other dismissive characterization. The contextual domain is also where true leadership is generated since genuine leadership is closely related to vision. Transcendent leadership—the quality that allows leaders to expand their consciousness beyond the existing physical paradigm—permits leaders to embrace the spiritual as a routine part of their style.

If business is ever going to have a shot at getting "out of its own box," *business leaders and business thought leaders must get familiar with the contextual domain.*

We in the West like our models simple, easy-to-comprehend, and tangible. The intangible and more complex matters turn us off in business. *This must change!*

Each of us must find our own path to achieve a personal transformation in order that we can accept paradigm shifts on an organizational level. But, there's no easy five-step model or twelve phases or seven habits or any other simplistic way to tell you how to achieve this change in how we think.

After all, we are dealing with a complex world, filled with increasingly complex systems. So we need to start thinking more systemically, more complexly. And, please note that I'm not saying more *complicated.* I'm saying more *complex.*

Where it Begins

Once we change our thinking, we will all know what needs to be done in the domains of form and content. After all, we have plenty of technology and knowledge at our disposal. Once we believe that a better future is possible, see what it can be and know what we want to make happen, we will have the know-how to do it. But it starts with the way we think and the consciousness we bring to our lives and our work.

We do not lack for information. What we lack is consciousness. What we lack is wisdom.

No plan, no model, no concept can cause a real and meaningful transformation. Only people can, people who bring a new consciousness to the old problems—just like Einstein pointed out earlier this century. The people who bring in this new consciousness need not have great credentials or positions of tremendous influence. All they need is a genuine intention and willingness to think differently.

The new leaders for the new millennium will be ordinary people doing extraordinary things, working in concert with other ordinary folks.

To achieve this transformation, to shape this historic paradigm shift, we need to start somewhere, sometime, with someone.

Where does it start? It starts *here....*

When does it start? It starts *now...*

Who starts it? *You and I* do!

Appendices

Appendix A: The 21ˢᵗ Century Agenda for Business

Appendix B: "Design a Better Future" article from *Industry Week* magazine

Appendix C: Resources

"Our real values are expressed in our actions, in what we do and how we do them. Our actions never contradict our values: our actions are our values."

—Robert Rabbin, *author, The Sacred Hub*

Appendix A

The 21st-Century Agenda
for Business

A Global Resolution for New Corporate Values and Priorities

"Problems cannot be solved at the same level of consciousness that created them."

— Albert Einstein

Social researcher Paul Ray discovered that over 44 million people in the U.S. alone now subscribe to new values and ways of relating to each other, the environment, success and spirituality. These findings were first published in 1994 and the numbers were still growing. This suggests a global trend toward - as well as a growing receptivity for - new values and priorities for business. This Agenda may serve as a venue for some of these millions as well as their counterparts in other countries to express their endorsement for these new values and priorities.

The tenets* of this Agenda are aligned with the values and priorities described by many visionaries who have foreseen new futures for humanity. These visions include, but are not limited to, Willis Harman's "Second Copernican Revolution;" Peter Russell's "Age of Consciousness;" Riane Eisler's "Partnership Model," Robert Greenleaf's "Servant Leadership;" Michael Ray's "New Paradigm;" Peter Senge's "Learning Organization;" Dee Hock's "Chaordic Organization;" Rolf Osterberg's "Corporate Renaissance;" Taichi Sakaiya's "Knowledge-Value Era," Charles Handy's "Age of Paradox;" Alvin Toffler's "Third Wave;" Karl Henrik-Robert's "The Natural Step" and others who have advocated similar possibilities.

This document has been drafted by an informal group of people in business who are concerned about the state of the world, the relationship between the business community and the rest of global society, and who hold a visionary and transcendent perspective on life and work. People and organizations who support the tenets of this resolution are invited to add their names as Co-signers to this document.

What follows includes:

- A short Preamble that provides a context for the Agenda and a description for how to register as a Co-signer.
  - The Resolution itself.
  - The list of current Co-signers.

---

*tenet: a principle, belief, or doctrine generally held to be true...one held in common by members of an organization, movement, or profession (Webster).

The Preamble

Business has become the most dominant institution on Earth. Within the global business community, there is a spiritual renaissance fermenting. Many people are calling for "conscious organizations" - companies that embody principles of interconnectedness, stewardship, compassion and global ecology in their business dealings. Over the past few years, *The Wall Street Journal, Business Week, Chief Executive* and numerous other business periodicals have featured this trend in business philosophy.

Heads of state are advocating a "third way" economic system - neither communism nor the current version of capitalism - but a new system that engenders a more compassionate, generous and sustainable world. To those who have an awareness of these trends, it is obvious that something very big is underway - a societal transformation on a massive scale - and business can play a major role.

Growing numbers of working men and women have a deep yearning to connect with others who share their desire to see business take a responsible and constructive role in this transformation. Some have formed or joined groups or networks where they experience some sense of community. Others participate in Internet discussions groups, or virtual communities. Some have organized conferences, retreats and other gatherings where these "communities of interest" can come together and discuss common issues and ideas. But how can we express this interest and support and endorse these new values and priorities acting together as a whole?

Add Your Name and Make a Difference

Co-signing this Agenda is a way for people to add their name to a resolution that can change the world. There is no expense or ongoing obligation. There are no leaders to follow, no events to attend, no rules or hierarchies of membership, no membership dues to pay and no governance to contend with. All you do is add your name to a statement of values and priorities that you agree with.

That's it!

Interested?

Please look over the following Resolution and see if you support it. If you agree with these principles, values and priorities, agree to support and abide by them, and commit to using them as a guide in your own business activities, then consider becoming a Co-signer. Simply register by adding your name, city, country and title or affiliation to those who already stand behind it.

The Spirit of Becoming a Co-Signer

By becoming a Co-signer you will have added something very important to this public Agenda - your name. With your name you lend your reputation, your credential, your stance for what's important, your intention, your vision and your commitment to making major changes in how business interacts with the rest of society and the Earth in the future. Everyone adding their name and business credential will be adding further legitimacy to these values. Please do not use your "signature" to promote yourself. We are all *giving* to this project without expectation of *getting* anything from it, other than a better world.

To Become a Co-signer

Due to Co-signer verification concerns, only people with their own email addresses and Web access can directly co-sign the Agenda. To become a Co-signer, read the document and complete the registration form. Please note that the number of characters for your title/ affiliation is limited to 125 letters or spaces (see existing Co-signers below for examples). Contact information for Co-signers will not be published.

Inform Others

If you know others who have Web access and who may wish to sign on, let them know where they can view the Agenda for themselves so they can join in. You are urged to promote the Agenda as widely as possible through your own networks. Let your Internet colleagues know about it if you think they'll join in. If you have a personal or company homepage on the Web, consider linking it to the Agenda's homepage so your Internet visitors can easily find the Agenda for themselves. You may use the sample invitation to inform others of its existence and invite them to become Co-signers.

The Resolution

We the people who have co-signed below agree with the tenets included herein and commit to the following vision: *a world in which the global business community serves society in ways that are life-affirming, sustainable, humanistic and responsible for positively influencing the future evolution of humanity.*

Whereas:

1. We acknowledge that: a) humanity faces grave crises on many fronts that cannot be averted through scientific technology alone; b) the industrialization of the developing and undeveloped world is push-

ing these crises to a point of irreversibility; and c) a new consciousness is required to solve these problems;

2.We affirm that all of humanity is interconnected;

3.We acknowledge that, at present, the business community is one of the primary influences - good or bad - on society, its values and its priorities;

4.We believe that, having such a profound influence, business has an opportunity to assume a responsible and constructive role in the transformation of society and that it has a social purpose as well as an economic purpose;

5.We recognize that many organizations are decentralizing as they realize the value of collaboration as a means of dealing with exploding complexity in the marketplace and that this decentralization represents a movement from hierarchy to community;

6.We recognize that business practices, values and priorities can be changed;

7.We believe that the real power and capabilities of business can be unleashed and expanded by recognizing powers greater than the physical sciences, and that love, generosity, compassion and non-denominational spiritual values have a place in this new paradigm for business;

8.We realize that such a major change will occur when there is a transformation in the core mindset of people throughout the industrialized world and in those nations which are aspiring to "catch up with the west"; and that business possesses the transformative power to achieve this;

9.We recognize that a post-Industrial Age paradigm is being called forth, one that invites radically new thought and an openness to ideas previously disallowed from business philosophy and leadership thinking; and

10. We realize that traditional thinking about the purpose of business maintains the status quo and that transformation can only occur if this thinking and the assumptions underlying it are challenged.

Be it resolved that:

In recognition of these acknowledgements, realizations and beliefs, we the undersigned hereby commit ourselves and our organizations to the following:

1.Affirm Life: engage in commerce so as to support, affirm and nurture life and Nature, creating a positive future and a long-term sustainable world; cease promotion of excessive and needless consumption;

2.Balance Economic Focus: recognize that making a profit is a necessity for a business and not its only purpose for existing; employ socially-and environmentally -just financial measurements; become more aware of how much economics dominates our society;

3.Act With Integrity: recognize the interconnectedness of all things and that each human is a part of a larger whole, so that holistic thinking with integrity, truthfulness and honesty follow;

4.Be Socially Responsible: in a spirit of stewardship, engage in everyday business with awareness of the company's impact upon Nature and humanity, implementing social and environmental audits so that true costs for all utilized resources can be established;

5.Honor Community: recognize all stakeholders who are affected by the business, including employees, vendors, customers, owners and stockholders, the environment and local communities where the business is located; contribute to the spirit of healthy community among all stakeholders by valuing them individually and as a whole; promote dialogue and true conversation among the parties;

6.Value Everyone: honor and respect every person regardless of their differences; acknowledge and recognize each individual; recognize the value of diversity;

7.Respect the Complete Human: utilize and honor the human spirit as well as the rational and physical human; value aesthetics and the immaterial aspects of work as well as the economic and material aspects;

8.Honor and Respect Emotions: support and encourage the understanding and healthy expression of all human emotions;

9.Speak Out Publicly: explicitly promote these values and priorities to peers and colleagues so more and more people and companies can make similar commitments thereby contributing to a more positive future for everyone.

NOTE: A list of co-signers follows the Resolution portion of the Agenda. To see the entire Agenda homepage, go to http://www.the-agenda.net and join the other co-signers already listed.

Appendix B

Industry Week magazine   May 6 1996   "On the Edge" series:

"Design a Better Future"

by Perry Pascarella

A businessman all his adult life—promoting bikers, car drivers, and real-estate investments - John Renesch formed Sterling & Stone in San Francisco in 1989 as a merchant banking company to help businesses that were trying to bring about a new awareness in the business world. When a friend with the capital didn't come through, he turned to producing The New Leaders *newsletter. He later added the imprint New Leaders Press to publish such books as* The New Entrepreneurs, Leadership in a New Era, *and* Rediscovering the Soul of Business, *and one now in production:* The New Bottom Line. *Renesch flips through his mental Rolodex to line up authors around the world for these compilations on leadership issues. During 1990-92 he also served as managing director of the World Business Academy, whose mission is to provide opportunities for people in business to engage in meaningful conversation about business' leadership role in society.*

Sterling & Stone promises in its mission statement that it will "en-courage the human spirit in the workplace and the emerging of a new consciousness in business."

With the motor-sports business a distant part of his varied past, John Renesch now runs in the biggest race of all. He is convinced we have to break through to a higher consciousness—to the next step in human evolution—before our system collapses. And he believes that business bears most of the responsibility for leading that change. A shift in consciousness is beginning, he believes. "The honeymoon is over for the industrial age. There is growing disenchantment with the industrial paradigm. We are seeing the price we pay for having industrialized the human being. I think the business community has become very good at doing one thing, but very dysfunctional from a holistic perspective. Business organizations have made survival an art form, but look at the trail of blood they leave behind: people demeaned, people asked to do things that go against their conscience, people overworked, people stressed out." In addition, many are questioning old assumptions about our major addiction to consuming. "We buy things we don't need, and we have more choices of product than we need. If this country is consuming half the resources of the planet, and the rest of the world is aspiring to be as consumptive as we are, it ain't going to work. If they get what they want, there's going to be total taxation of our resources. We, as the most consumptive society in the world, are going to have to change drastically our pattern of consumption.

"It could sound like I'm antibusiness, but I've been in business since I was 18. Most of the time I had to make something happen. I was the entrepreneur.

"A lot of companies are going to have to get even smaller. A lot of companies are going to die, and some of them know it. There are companies that shouldn't be in business anymore. They've done their thing. They need a total redefinition of their mission. They should take all their talent and do something else with it." Smiling as he considers a breakthrough possibility, he asks, "What if we took all of our capital, all of our resources, all of our people and put them into something else that society really needs?"

More and more people are sensing the system's failure to satisfy them, Renesch believes. "Every system that was designed to provide security for the American individual is in collapse. You cannot be assured of a job. You aren't going to be guaranteed health care. The legal system is on its head. Every system that we set up to provide positive reinforcement and security is in dysfunction.

"The pain and anguish of the late '80s and early '90s prompted people to ask deeper questions. As a nation, we got as opulent as you could get, but there was still a hollow spot. It's like the song: 'Is that all there is?'" Renesch himself was part of the money craze of the '80s. In the mid-'70s he experienced what he calls a mid-life crisis. "I decided I wanted to make some real money. I formed a real-estate-investment company as a partner. Raising money became a big part of my life. We were getting fabulous returns. But by 1983 I felt it was time to get started on doing something really good for the world."

For Renesch, the world crisis is more than a matter of conserving resources. He aims way beyond preserving physical resources to engaging the human spirit. "The spirit is that spark that tells us we're alive. When work is meaningful, when one's passion is being involved in his or her work, there's a sense of aliveness, a sense of the human spirit thriving," he says.

Environmentalists work to postpone the limits to consumption, but Renesch strives to hasten a shift in consciousness—a major transformation. "Too many of us are spending our time paying the mortgage, feeling the need to numb out in some way—watching TV, drawing away from people, substance abuse—just putting in our time. The American Dream has gotten really distorted," Renesch says. "It's a consumer-based dream. The American Dream of the founding fathers was very spiritually based. Somewhere after World War II, the American Dream changed.

"I think it's appropriate that this country be the source of a renaissance of responsible business, because we are the first ones to see the downside of the dream," he explains. Business is in the best position to lead a transformation, he is convinced, because it has a "disproportionate share of influence on society. With that much control over people's lives it's inherent—a kind of natural law—that you've got responsibility for it. In the days of Adam Smith in the 1700s you had a presumption that you had a moral society. You had a presumption that there was a conscience at work. Over the years, we have done so much in the way of legislation and the rule of law that we've unconsciously evolved to a state where everything is O.K. unless it's illegal. So there's no longer an inner moral code. The moral compass went out the window, and it became a game of exploiting loopholes. Our conscience has atrophied."

Major social transformation and an awakening to a higher consciousness has begun, Renesch believes. "Society is changing its mindset from competition, scarcity, short-term [goals], and exploitation to sustainability, connectedness, cooperation, and responsibility of the haves for the have-nots. People are feeling an interconnectedness with the world."

He feels a calling to support this emerging new paradigm and accelerate it to avoid a world crisis. "The species for the first time in its history can annihilate itself or transcend. It is either going to kill itself off or go to the next step of evolution, which is this divine consciousness, becoming connected holistically with everybody. We're on the brink of an evolutionary shift. What could be more exciting than human beings leaving their skin of separateness?" In this rise to a oneness, Renesch sees modern computer/communications technology as a gap-filler. "At some point we may not even need the hardware," he muses.

"You can't tell when a shift is going to happen. It may take millions of years getting ready, and suddenly it happens. This consciousness shift is already happening in many places, in many stages.

"There's a lot of transformation going on very privately within people as they meditate, pray, and engage in relationships that influence them. I believe there will be a series of out-of-the-closet-ness, where, once a certain amount of mass of agreement is formed within individuals, somebody will say something and everybody is going to be talking about it as if they have been there all along. All of a sudden, something that was very private and dear will come out like it has always been out because it has been within people for so long.

"There's a more spiritual side to the human spirit, too — the relationship that we humans have with the divine. People are plugging in to universal life, the divine, the sacred. But the popularity of literature on soul and spirituality in business will pass soon," Renesch warns. The term "spiritual" gets muddied and confused with spiritualism and spiritualists. He prefers to use the term "consciousness" to include "awareness beyond the little self to the entire species and beyond, an awareness, responsibility, and the divine dimension."

Everyone a leader

The new paradigm includes the concept that we are all leaders. By leadership, Renesch means we all have stewardship for the organization. "When you see something that needs to be done you ascend to leadership in that incident. When that's done you go back to being not a follower, necessarily, but *one of.* It's a matter of being responsible. If you're responsible as a forklift operator, you're a leader when you see that there's a way to be more efficient. Typically, what happens is we say, 'It's not my job.'

"It's still a mistake to think of leadership coming from the top. The system is set up to recognize people at the top. We still have this star, guru, celebrity thing about people." As a result, there are huge numbers of people below the top who say, "If only we could get them to change," referring to the established leaders. And, at the same time, people at the top lament that they can't get people below to change. "People at the bottom have historically thought of themselves as the disempowered. 'We're only the workers,' they assume.

"I'm not convinced you can empower anybody. People have to empower themselves, and there has to be a climate or texture or context of allowing for that. When people say, 'We're going to empower our employees,' it's the same hierarchy; it's just talking a different language. That's saying, 'I want to empower them because I want to get more out of them.'" Renesch believes, however, that an increasing number of managers are actually walking the talk, and, in the lower ranks, more people are taking more responsible roles. In fact, the idea of taking personal responsibility for one's life, work, and the planet started in the '60s and '70s, he points out.

"I don't think we'll ever end up with a CEO-less organization," he admits. "There'll still be somebody at the top. For them to stay empowered, however, they are going to have to recognize there's leadership throughout the organization, and they will have to honor leadership from wherever it comes. Leadership must emerge from all levels of our organizations if they are going to survive.

"Transformative leaders are getting the job done, given their position in the organization, but there's a transformative quality about the way they are doing it so that other people working with them feel empowered without management empowering them."

Cheerleaders

Out on the leading edge, calling for "outrageous leaders of change," Renesch is dedicated to building a critical mass of people who can cause a revolution in what we can be. "The advocates of transformation in the business world for the most part are very demure," he is sorry to say. "They are very scholarly, very quiet, soft spoken. They are not cheerleaders. If we had more people speaking more courageously on what they think is right, there might be far more agreement for that rightness than they ever imagined. It might be that everybody is waiting for somebody to stick their neck out. I think what we have is a huge conspiracy of silence in the business community, just as we do in most systems that are dysfunctional."

Renesch sees his mission as providing products that speak up— that inform, inspire, and connect people who have a new awareness in the business world. Reading about leaders shows them they are not alone. "In the business world there's a yearning for connecting with like-minded kindred spirits who are as concerned with the way things are going—the quality of life, the pressures, the pace of life," he explains. "The whole quality of one's humanness seems to be getting quashed." He wants to provide reinforcement material so that people can be advocates of change in their organizations.

But Renesch is not Pollyanna-ish about the future we can build. The world doesn't have to be full of struggle and pain with occasional acts of goodness. While it will never be perfect, we could make it "a world of goodness with random acts of violence."

He suspects, "If most of us were in a state of consciousness, really in touch with our passion, there's some divine plan out there that says that if everybody follows their passion, there would be just enough carpenters, just enough publishers, just enough policemen, it would all work out."

Who knows how much we can improve our lot and realize who we are? "Everything we have done up to now in history has been a projection of the past. The future has always been related to the past. But," says Renesch, "we are leaving that paradigm, and the future is going to be the future we envision—the future we create for ourselves.

Appendix C

RESOURCES

Business for Social Responsibility
609 Mission Street, 2nd Floor
San Francisco, CA 94105
415-537-0888
mail @ bsr.org

European Bahai' Business Forum
35 Ave Jean Jaures
Chambery 73000
France
+33 0479 962272
c/o Secretariat, George Starcher
GS12 @ calva.net

Foundation for Conscious Evolution
P.O. 4698
Santa Barbara, CA 93140
805-884-9212
mail @ peaceroom.org

Genesis: The Foundation for the Universal Human
P.O. Box 2144
Redway, CA 95560
800-454-SOUL
soulsource @ zukav.com

Institute of Noetic Sciences
475 Gate Five Road, #300
Sausalito, CA 94965
415-331-5650
membership @ noetic.org

Net Impact (formerly Students for Responsible Business)
609 Mission Street, Third Floor
San Francisco, CA 94105
415-778-8366
mail @ net-impact.net

Social Venture Network
P.O. Box 29221
San Francisco, CA 94129
415-561-6501
svn @ wenet.net

The 21st Century Agenda for Business: A Global Resolution for New
Corporate Values and Priorities
Unattended Web site only: http: // 165.90.46.230 / THE-AGENDA

The Club of Budapest Foundation
Szentharomsag ter 6
H-1014 Budapest
Hungary
011-361-175-1885
budapest_klub @ mail.matav.hu

The Society for Organizational Learning
617-492-6260
Web Site: www. sol-ne.org
contact @ sol-ne.org

World Business Academy
P.O. Box 50450
Pasadena, CA 91115
626-403-3358
wba @ well.com

World Future Society
7910 Woodmont Ave. #450
Bethesda, MD 20814
301-656-8274
info @ wfs.org

BIBLIOGRAPHY

"America's World," *The Economist*, October 23, 1999

"A Nation Divided," Mortimer Zuckerman, *U.S. News & World Report*, October 18, 1999

Anderson, Ray C., *Mid-Course Correction: Toward A Sustainable Enterprise: The Interface Model*, Atlanta, GA, Peregrinzilla Press, 1998

Berenson, David, "A Systemic View of Spirituality: God and Twelve Step Programs as Resources in Family Therapy," in *Addiction and Spirituality: A Multidisciplinary Approach*, O.J. Morgan and M. Jordan (eds), Chalice Press, St. Louis, 1999

"Coming Together, Ten Years On," *The Economist*, November 13, 1999

"Corporate Futures: An Interview with David Korten and Paul Hawken," *Yes! A Journal for Positive Futures*, Positive Futures Network, Summer 1999

Dalai Lama, *Ethics for the New Millennium*, New York, Riverhead Books, 1999

Deming, W. Edwards, *The New Economics: For Industry, Government, Education*, Cambridge, MA, MIT, 1993

Didsbury, Jr, Howard, Preface and Introduction, *Frontiers of the 21st Century: Prelude to the New Millennium*, Bethesda, MD, World Future Society, 1999

Drucker, Peter, *Landmarks of Tomorrow*, New Brunswick, NJ, Transaction Publishers, 1996

Emery, Stewart, "A Conversation with Norman Lear," in *Leadership in a New Era* (ed. John Renesch), San Francisco, New Leaders Press, 1994

"Find a Place to Stand," by Lynne Twist, *Yes! A Journal for Positive Futures*, Positive Futures Network, Fall 1999

Fox, Matthew, *The Reinvention of Work: A New Vision of Livelihood for*

Our Time, Harper San Francisco, 1994

Friedman, Milton, "The Social Responsibility of Business is to Increase its Profits," *The New York Times Magazine*, September 13, 1970

Fritz, Robert. T*he Path of Least Resistance*, Fawcett-Columbine, New York, 1989

Handy, Charles, *The Hungry Spirit*, Broadway Books, New York, 1998

Harman, Willis, *Global Mind Change: The Promise of the 21st Century*, Berrett-Koehler Publishers and Institute of Noetic Sciences, San Francisco, 1998

Harvey, Jerry, *The Abilene Paradox And Other Meditations on Management*, Lexington Books, New York, 1988

Hock, Dee, *The Birth of the Chaordic Age*, Berrett-Koehler Publishers, San Francisco, 1999

Hubbard, Barbara Marx, *Conscious Evolution: Awakening the Power of Our Social Potential*, New World Library, Novato, CA, 1998

Kurtzman, Joel, *The Death of Money*, Simon & Schuster, New York, 1993

Land, George and Beth Jarman, *Breakpoint and Beyond: Mastering the Future Today*, Harper Collins, New York, 1992

Laszlo, Ervin, *3rd Millennium: The Challenge and the Vision*, Gaia Books Ltd., London, 1997

Laszlo, Ervin, *Choice: Evolution or Extinction?* Jeremy P. Tarcher/Putnam Books, New York, 1994

Leonard, George, "Taking the Hit as a Gift," *Review No. 49*, Institute of Noetic Sciences, August - November, 1999

Liberty, Larry, *Leadership Wisdom: A Guide to Producing Extraordinary Results*, Carmichael Printing, Carmichael, CA, 1990

Maslow, Abraham, *Motivation and Personality*, Harper & Row, New York, 1970

Muller, Robert, "The Absolute Urgent Need for Proper Earth Government," *Frontiers of the 21st Century: Prelude to the New Millennium*, Bethesda, MD, World Future Society, 1999

"New Report Anticipates Cultural Revitalization" (about Paul Ray's research), *The New Leaders* newsletter, November/December 1995

"Oprah Winfrey Show," ABC-TV, July 13, 1999

Pascarella, Perry, "Design a Better Future," *Industry Week*, May 6, 1996

Rabbin, Robert, *Invisible Leadership: Igniting the Soul at Work*, Acropolis Books, Lakewood, CO, 1998

Renesch, John, "The Conscious Organization," *Business Spirit Journal*, August, 1999

Renesch, John, "New Leaders for a New Future: The New Business Cosmology," *World Futures*, January, 1998

Renesch, John (ed), *The New Bottom Line: Bring Heart & Soul to Business*, New Leaders Press, San Francisco, 1996

Roddick, Anita, *Body and Soul: Profits With Principles*, New York, Crown Publishers, 1991

Russell, Peter, "Mysterious Light: A Scientist's Odyssey," *IONS Review No. 50*, December 1999 - March 2000, Institute of Noetic Sciences

Russell, Peter, *The Global Brain Awakens: Our Next Evolutionary Leap*, Global Brain, Inc., Palo Alto, CA, 1995

Schwartz, Peter, Peter Leyden and Joel Hyatt, *The Long Boom: A Vision for the Coming Age of Prosperity*, Perseus Books, Reading, MA, 1999

Senge, Peter M., *The Fifth Discipline: The Art & Practice of The Learning Organization*, Douleday/Currency, New York, 1990

"The Silicon Seduction," *San Francisco Magazine*, September, 1999

Thurow, Lester, *The Future of Capitalism: How Today's Economic Forces Shape Tomorrow's World*, William Morrow and Company, New York, 1996

Williamson, Marianne, *A Return to Love*, Harper Collins, San Francisco, 1996

Zukav, Gary. *The Seat of the Soul*, Simon and Schuster, New York, 1989

"Examining your life is an ongoing process which you can count on having around for the rest of your life, so long as you remain committed to your spiritual growth."

—John E. Renesch

ABOUT THE AUTHOR

John E. Renesch is a San Francisco writer, futurist, and business philosopher. From 1990 to 1997 he served as Editor-in-Chief of *The New Leaders* business newsletter. From 1990 to early 1992 he also was Managing Director of the World Business Academy, an international association focused on new paradigms for commerce. Prior to these positions, he was a founder or co-founder of several businesses, including a real estate investment company and two securities broker-dealers where he served as Managing Director and President respectively. He currently serves on the editorial board for Berrett-Koehler Publishers, the World 2000 project advisory board for the World Future Society, and the board of trustees for The Club of Budapest Foundation, dedicated to the advancement of planetary consciousness. John is a radio commentator for Whole News, a division of Wisdom Radio, an affiliate of the Wisdom Networks which broadcast uplifting programs via satellite and the Internet.

He has created a dozen business anthologies on progressive subjects, including consciousness, intuition and leadership. He is the creator of "The ARC Masters Series with John Renesch" - a monthly series of book excerpts for business leaders who are interested in personal development and introspection.

Over three hundred authors have contributed to twelve anthologies which he has compiled since 1990. John is also an international keynote speaker, having addressed audiences in Tokyo, Seoul, London, Brussels, Budapest as well as many cities throughout the U.S. He spends some of his time delivering keynotes to groups who are interested in his ideas.

For a free subscription to his electronic newsletter - *Aha!: the E-Newsletter for the Awakening Workplace* - or for more information about his work, visit his homepage on the Web at www .Renesch .com. To contact him by email: John @ Renesch .com; or by voicemail: 415-437-6974.

YOUR NAME CAN MAKE A DIFFERENCE

Join in this Internet resolution for doing business in a whole new way!

This is neither a petition nor a chain letter; it is a declaration of values and priorities that the co-signers support and advocate. Add your name and make a difference.

* * * * * * * * * * * * * * *

The 21st-Century Agenda for Business
A Global Referendum for New Corporate Values and Priorities

Take a stand. Put your name on the line.
It's quick, easy and can make a big difference.
Co-sign and join others who advocate a better future.

Go to:

http://www.the-agenda.net

Read the Agenda.
If you accept its tenets and wish to become a co-signer, add your name to those who have already endorsed it.
Then, as a co-signer, spread the word
to your colleagues, friends, co-workers and peers
who hold similar ideals for business' role in the world.

It can't hurt.

But it sure could help!

There is no cost, hidden or otherwise, to signing the Agenda. Co-signers will not be solicited as a result of signing the Agenda. While the Agenda is hosted on a commercial site, there are no commercial aspects to this public document. It is owned by no one, created collaboratively by several hundred people from several dozen countries.

Printed in the United States
3221